THE TURBULENT 60s

1967

**Other books in the
Turbulent 60s series:**

THE TURBULENT 60s

1967

Norman Loukes, *Book Editor*

Bruce Glassman, *Vice President*
Bonnie Szumski, *Publisher*
Scott Barbour, *Managing Editor*
David M. Haugen, *Series Editor*

**GREENHAVEN
PRESS** ®

THOMSON
— ★ —
GALE

San Diego • Detroit • New York • San Francisco • Cleveland
New Haven, Conn. • Waterville, Maine • London • Munich

Cover credit: © AP/Wide World Photos
Library of Congress, 21, 35, 56, 63, 88
National Archives, 79

LIBRARY OF CONGRESS CATALOGING-IN-PUBLICATION DATA

1967 / Norman Loukes, book editor.
    p. cm. — (The turbulent 60s)
  Includes bibliographical references and index.
  ISBN 0-7377-1838-2 (lib. : alk. paper) — ISBN 0-7377-1839-0 (pbk. : alk. paper)
    1. United States—History—1961–1969—Sources. 2. Nineteen sixty-seven, A.D.—Sources. I. Loukes, Norman. II. Turbulent 60s.
  E846.A185 2004
  973.923—dc22   2003061611

Printed in the United States of America

CONTENTS

FOREWORD

The 1960s were a period of immense change in America. What many view as the complacency of the 1950s gave way to increased radicalism in the 1960s. The newfound activism of America's youth turned an entire generation against the social conventions of their parents. The rebellious spirit that marked young adulthood was no longer a stigma of the outcast but rather a badge of honor among those who wanted to remake the world. And in the 1960s, there was much to rebel against in America. The nation's involvement in Vietnam was one of the catalysts that helped galvanize young people in the early 1960s. Another factor was the day-to-day Cold War paranoia that seemed to be the unwelcome legacy of the last generation. And for black Americans in particular, there was the inertia of the civil rights movement that, despite seminal victories in the 1950s, had not effectively countered the racism still plaguing the country. All of these concerns prompted the young to speak out, to decry the state of the nation that would be their inheritance.

The 1960s, then, may best be remembered for its spirit of confrontation. The student movement questioned American imperialism, militant civil rights activists confronted their elders over the slow progress of change, and the flower children faced the nation's capitalistic greed and conservative ethics and opted to create a counterculture. There was a sense of immediacy to all this activism, and people put their bodies on the line to bring about change. Although there were reactionaries and conservative holdouts, the general feeling was that a united spirit of resistance could stop the inevitability of history. People could shape their own destinies, and together they could make a better world. As sixties chronicler Todd Gitlin writes, "In the Sixties it seemed especially true that History with a capital H had come down to earth, either interfering with life or making it possible: and that within History, or threaded through it, people were living with a supercharged density: lives were bound up with one another, making claims on one another, drawing one another into the common project."

Perhaps not everyone experienced what Gitlin describes, but few would argue that the nation as a whole was left untouched by the radical notions of the times. The women's movement, the civil rights movement, and the antiwar movement left indelible marks. Even the hippie movement left behind a relaxed morality and a more ecological mindset. Popular culture, in turn, reflected these changes: Music became more diverse and experimental, movies adopted more adult themes, and fashion attempted to replicate the spirit of uninhibited youth. It seemed that every facet of American culture was affected by the pervasiveness of revolution in the 1960s, and despite the diversity of rebellions, there remained a sense that all were related to, as Gitlin puts it, "the common project."

Of course, this communal zeitgeist of the 1960s is best attributed to the decade in retrospect. The 1960s were not a singular phenomenon but a progress of individual days, of individual years. Greenhaven Press follows this rubric in The Turbulent Sixties series. Each volume of this series is devoted to the major events that define a specific year of the decade. The events are discussed in carefully chosen articles. Some of these articles are written by historians who have the benefit of hindsight, but most are contemporary accounts that reveal the complexity, confusion, excitement, and turbulence of the times. Each article is prefaced by an introduction that places the event in its historical context. Every anthology is also introduced by an essay that gives shape to the entire year. In addition, the volumes in the series contain time lines, each of which gives an at-a-glance structure to the major events of the topic year. A bibliography of helpful sources is also provided in each anthology to offer avenues for further study. With these tools, readers will better understand the developments in the political arena, the civil rights movement, the counterculture, and other facets of American society in each year. And by following the trends and events that define the individual years, readers will appreciate the revolutionary currents of this tumultuous decade—the turbulent sixties.

The Year of Empowerment

Nineteen sixty-seven was a tumultuous year of empowerment and awakening. Fueled by the events of an already turbulent decade, the year witnessed citizens taking an increasing interest in the actions of their government and its policies, both foreign and domestic. Mounting casualties in Vietnam, continuing racial tensions, and a burgeoning counterculture movement brought together many people who were dissatisfied with the status quo in America. The coming together of these people— especially the large youth movement—led to expressions of peaceful ideals juxtaposed with disturbing displays of violence. As "hippies" celebrated the Summer of Love, racial tensions boiled over into riots in several major cities. War protesters marched on Washington and burned draft cards in Oakland, California. High-profile public figures such as Muhammad Ali, Martin Luther King Jr., and Senator Eugene McCarthy gave support to the growing belief that the United States should bring an end to military involvement in Vietnam. All these various protest movements found their voices and proclaimed enough was enough. A feeling of unity and empowerment swept over the dissatisfied and the disenchanted and marked 1967 as the year in which a large section of Americans took a stand against their government and their society.

Resistance to the Vietnam War

Under President Lyndon B. Johnson, U.S. commitment to Vietnam rose dramatically. By the end of 1967 almost five hundred thousand U.S. troops were stationed in the small Southeast Asian country. Over the course of the year, nine thousand American troops would die in battle. The rising death toll, combined with the Johnson administration's rigid determination to win the conflict by sheer force of numbers, began to sway public opinion dramatically against the war. As historian Stanley Karnow notes,

> The seemingly straightforward conflict soon degenerated into a protracted, exhausting, indecisive war of attrition that increasingly appeared to be futile. President Johnson nevertheless persisted with expressions of determination and optimism—and U.S. troops continued to fight and die as the war generated its own momentum. As the struggle lengthened, American's faith in its invincibility faded.[1]

This air of invincibility was further challenged by large demonstrations in several large cities. In one large gathering in Washington, D.C., Abbie Hoffman led a colorful group of protesters in a whimsical attempt to levitate the Pentagon as a means of exorcising the demons within. Not so amusing were the clashes that followed soon after. On October 21, 1967, over one hundred thousand citizens gathered around the Lincoln Memorial, and some began to march toward the Pentagon. They were soon met by army troops and police. CIA director Richard Helms remembered that the police were expecting a fight: "I don't think there was any doubt that they took a look at that mob around the Pentagon and nobody liked the look of that at all. And I certainly least of all. I'd had experiences with mobs all over the world and I didn't like the look or sound of this one bit."[2] Arrests and bloodshed followed as demonstrators repeatedly attempted to rush the Pentagon.

Soon after the Washington gathering, Stop the Draft Week in Oakland, California, brought hundreds of people together to burn their draft cards in symbolic disapproval of the war. In growing numbers, Americans empowered with a sense that this war was wrong were beginning to exercise freedom of speech as never before. For the young people, the risk was high, since refusing a draft call was a federal offense. Other protests inspired by Stop the Draft Week were staged in other U.S. cities. Historian Tom Wells describes one student protest in Madison, Wisconsin, that was directed not at military recruiters, but at recruiters for Dow Chemical, a manufacturer of the chemical agent napalm which had been used with horrific effects in Vietnam.

> On the University of Wisconsin campus in Madison, a throng of students strode into the Commerce Building and proclaimed an

end to the job interviews being conducted there by recruiters from the Dow Chemical Company. They would leave when Dow's bagmen left. A university official initially agreed to shoo the recruiters away, but, when asked to put his commitment on paper, "lost his cool." In came the local police riot squad. Students were swiftly streaming out of the building, battered and dazed, only to be beaten again by a gauntlet of cops. The two thousand onlookers who had gathered outside, "smelling trouble as sure as any turkey buzzard," were furious at the wanton police violence. "Sieg Heil," they chanted, arms upward. Many were gassed. They pelted police with rocks and bricks. When Mace failed to make the protestors lethargic, the county sheriff's office dispatched a riot team with snarling dogs. The tired and bloodied crowd gradually disbanded.[3]

As public support for the Johnson administration waned due to the unpopularity of the war, it became increasingly obvious that someone would step forward to run for president as the antiwar candidate. Many expected Massachusetts senator Robert Kennedy to unite the voters as the peace candidate. However, Kennedy was slow to voice his acceptance of the role of peace candidate. Instead, Senator Eugene McCarthy of Minnesota announced on November 30 that he would run against Johnson and make ending the war part of his presidential platform. Stanley Karnow remarks, "Johnson was furious at the prospect of facing an anti-war candidate, and increasingly agitated at the large number of anti-war demonstrations that had erupted across the country."[4]

Ali Takes a Stand

The antiwar movement was also bolstered by the public pronouncements of two of America's most beloved figures, boxer Muhammad Ali and civil rights activist Martin Luther King Jr.

On the national and world stage of professional athletics, there have been few athletes that rival the natural athletic ability and acerbic wit of the immensely popular Ali. Born Cassius Clay, Ali changed his name after being indoctrinated into the Nation of Islam. In 1967 Ali held the title of undisputed heavyweight champion of the world in the physically and mentally demanding sport of professional boxing. He was then drafted for service in the U.S. Army. Ali refused to serve, however, because of his belief in nonviolence stemming from his Islamic faith. Ali's refusal to join the army sent shockwaves not only through the sporting world but also all over the nation. He was, at the time, the most recognizable figure to refuse mandatory military service. Voicing his opposition, Ali declared, "I ain't got no quarrel with them Vietcong."[5]

Ali faced legal consequences due to his choice, but he held firm to his belief in nonviolence. Despite the ramifications, Ali's decision inspired others to refuse military service and brought a touch of celebrity to the antiwar movement. According to biographer David Roenick: "As he had before and would again, Ali had showed his gift for intuitive action, for speed, and this time he was acting in a way that would characterize the era itself, a resistance to authority, an insistence that national loyalty was not automatic or absolute. His rebellion, which had started out as racial, had now widened in its shape."[6]

King Ties Vietnam to Civil Rights

Earlier in the decade King had become the symbolic head of the civil rights movement, leading many of the nonviolent protests that challenged the "separate but equal" segregation policies still lingering in the United States. But in 1967 King joined the antiwar movement. Although some critics viewed this shift in focus as potentially sapping the momentum of the civil rights movement, King insisted the two causes were related. In speaking out against the Vietnam War, he brought to light his concerns that Vietnam was becoming a deathbed for lower-class American men, including large numbers of African Americans. King also lamented the government's concern with the war in Asia when it had yet to win the fight against poverty and racism at home. According to King, the Vietnam War was a civil rights disaster for African Americans:

> It (the war) was sending their sons and their brothers and their husbands to fight and to die and in extraordinarily high proportions relative to the rest of the population. We were taking the black young men who had been crippled by our society and sending them eight thousand miles away to guarantee liberties in Southeast Asia which they had not found in southwest Georgia and East Harlem.[7]

Even as King was making the point that American interests in Vietnam were superseding the resolution of racial problems in the United States, violent race riots were erupting in major cities around the country. The feelings of frustration that blacks felt for decades were boiling over. As King pointed out, the strides made by the civil rights movement in the early 1960s were threatened by lingering feelings of racism, hostility, and the dismal economic cycle of poverty forced upon African Americans:

> The policy-makers of the white society have caused the darkness: they created discrimination; they created slums; they perpetuate unemployment, ignorance, and poverty. It is incontestable and deplorable that Negroes have committed crimes, but they are derivative crimes. They are born of the greater crimes of the white society. When we ask Negroes to abide by the law, let us also declare that the white man does not abide by law in the ghettos. Day in and day out he violate welfare laws to deprive the poor of their meager allotments; he flagrantly violates building codes and regulations; his police make a mockery of law; he violates laws on equal employment and education and the provisions for civic services. The slums are a handiwork of a handiwork of a vicious system of the white society; Negroes live in them, buy they do not make them, any more than a prisoner makes a prison.[8]

The Long, Hot Summer

Such were the social conditions that led to riots across the country in 1967. The summer of 1967 was labeled "The Long, Hot Summer" both for the intense heat and equally intense riots that plagued the Northeast and Midwest. Major cities such as Milwaukee, Newark, and Detroit witnessed some of the worst rioting. Angry, out-of-control rioters ravaged these cities, looting and murdering. Racial tensions between black citizens and police officers in the slums of Detroit had been building for years. When a disputed incident of police brutality occurred in the summer of 1967 at the Algiers Motel, these tensions hit the breaking point, leading to the riots that engulfed the city. The situation quickly escalated into a national emergency, and National Guard troops were called in to restore order to a seven-day ordeal that saw hundreds killed or arrested and millions of dollars in property damaged. Many cities like Detroit were scarred for decades, as much of the remaining white population of the inner cities fled to the suburbs, a trend often referred to as the "white flight."

As Martin Luther King Jr. argued, these riots were the result of decades of frustration by those living in the ghettos and slums of the inner cities. Although African Americans made great strides in terms of civil rights earlier in the 1960s, many of the economic and social problems remained. Unplanned and uncontrolled, the riots can be looked upon as an effort by the inner-city black community to empower itself—sending the message that blacks would not settle for mere lip service when it came to racial equality.

As riots flared, a more organized form of black empowerment was taking shape in the ghettos of Oakland, California. One of the most influential political groups of the late sixties, the Black Panthers first gained notoriety by storming the California State Building on May 2, 1967, armed—legally—with rifles and shotguns. Distrusting the government and law enforcement, their message was that black Americans would no longer idly suffer abuse at the hands of whites, whether being harassed by bigots or shot down by police officers. Although the Panthers were often disregarded as a militant fringe group, they served notice that African Americans would no longer be silent victims of white oppression.

A Counterculture

While many citizens empowered themselves by giving voice to their social and political views, other sought merely to distance themselves from the doldrums of what they saw as a stagnant society. The movement to "drop out" of society was increasingly evident in 1967 in the San Francisco Bay area. A convergence of social and artistic ideals occurred in the Haight-Ashbury section of San Francisco as musicians, poets, reformers, and political malcontents pooled their ideas to create a utopian view of what American could be. This movement, popularly dubbed the "hippie movement," was formed in reaction to perceived social ills—the war, racism, consumerism, and the Cold War mind-set. To mark their rebellion, the hippies and other fringe groups embraced colorful clothing, experimental music, psychedelic drugs, and a less repressive view of sexuality.

Mainstream America did not know what to make of the Haight's carnival atmosphere, but the libertine values—viewed as licentious—were deemed dangerous especially in the hands of the nation's youth. As author Blair Jackson remarks:

> *Time* and *Newsweek*, *Look* and *Life*, and all the major television networks covered the rise of the San Francisco Counterculture with varying degrees of befuddlement. This was, after all, some-

thing genuinely new in this country, a cultural and generational rebellion of unparalleled scope and seriousness. Though it was easy for main stream Americans to chuckle at the colorful external trappings of the revolution—the long hair, wild clothes, and jargon-filled lexicon, not to mention that noise that these kids call music—the majority of Americans truly believed that what they saw happening in the Haight, and maybe on a much smaller scale in their own cities and towns, was truly a threat to the American way of life.[9]

Unfortunately for some, the experimental drug use and promiscuous sexual behavior promoted by the popular culture of this era resulted in more problems than solutions. Such was the case in Haight-Ashbury. As a social historians Martin A. Lee and Bruce Shlain note, the rise and fall of the hippie culture in San Francisco was tied to its vices: "Although the straight had scarcely begun to notice what was happening, the psychedelic city-state was having its brief golden age. The energy was unmistakably sky-high; poets and dreamers had the upper hand. One way or another, it revolved around drugs."[10] The influx of people and increasing drug use caused the Summer of Love to be short-lived. In October 1967 citizens of the Haight marched down the street in a mock funeral ceremony renouncing the "death of the hippie." Haight-Ashbury, the home of freethinkers and utopian visonaries, had become inundated with the problems associated with drug abuse, sexually transmitted diseases, and an influx of outsiders who wanted to reap the fruits of the alternative scene. As musician Jerry Garcia lamented, "There were a lot of people looking for the free ride. That's the death of any scene, when you have more drag energy than you have forward-going energy."[11]

From Empowerment to Rage

Protests, riots, and the rise of a unique cultural movement characterized the empowering effects of many of the events of 1967. However, the eventful year of 1967 came with severe growing pains. Lyndon Johnson's presidency would come to be characterized by the Vietnam War, which many Americans saw as spiraling out of control. Racism was still plaguing the nation, fomenting urban riots and engendering a growing sense of militancy and separatism. The counterculture movement also showed that America's youth were disillusioned with mainstream society and would stand against it. Although 1967 may have been empowering, it showed that tensions had finally reached the boiling point. When the hippie movement imploded, the Black Panthers' posturing proved ineffective, and the antiwar protests did not result in a swift end to the war, the sense of empowerment would become a backlash of rage that carried through the end of the 1960s.

Notes

1. Stanley Karnow, *Vietnam: A History.* New York: Penguin, 1997, p. 453.
2. Quoted in Tom Wells, *The War Within: American's Battle over Vietnam.* Berkeley: University of California Press, 1994, p. 197.
3. Wells, *The War Within,* p. 193.
4. Karnow, *Vietnam,* p. 478.
5. Quoted in David Roenick, *King of the World.* New York: Random House, 1998, p. 287.
6. Roenick, *King of the World,* p. 287.
7. Martin Luther King Jr., *The Trumpet of Conscience.* New York: Harper & Row, 1968, p. 23.
8. King, *The Trumpet of Conscience,* p. 8.
9. Blair Jackson, *Garcia: An American Life.* New York: Penguin, 2000, p. 131.
10. Martin A. Lee and Bruce Shlain, *The Complete Social History of LSD: The CIA, the Sixties, and Beyond.* New York: Grove, 1985, p. 145.
11. Quoted in Jackson, *Garcia,* p. 132.

Super Bowl I Begins a Cultural Phenomenon

By Steve Bisheff

In the fast-paced, high-stakes world of professional athletics, there is always another game to watch. But in the United States, every game is second to the AFC-NFC world championship game, known fondly as the "Super Bowl." Since the Super Bowl brought the American Football League together with the National Football League for the first time in Los Angeles in January 1967, the annual spectacle has grown into the premier yearly athletic contest. Advertisers shell out hundreds of millions of dollars every year in an attempt to reach the huge audience that watches the event annually.

A risky venture in its 1967 inception, the Super Bowl has transformed from a mere athletic championship into a cultural force that parallels America's fascination with professional sports and the athletes that play them. In the following 1996 article, journalist Steve Bisheff comments on the changes that have turned the Super Bowl from just a game into an annual tradition of epic proportions for sports fans.

TEMPE, Ariz. (1996): They will arrive in their private jets and stretch limos, play golf, get in a little tennis and attend cocktail parties in rooms larger than some football fields.

The Super Bowl has become Corporate America's game. But it wasn't always that way.

It wasn't always 2,500 members of the media shoving and jostling in front of some podium, straining to hear a quote from a strutting cornerback with three pounds of gold chains around his neck, either.

Super Bowl 30, meet Super Bowl 1. And oh yes, we understand if you two don't get along. After all, you really don't have very much in common.

Thirty seasons after this extravaganza has developed into the biggest sports event of the year, into a Sunday afternoon folkfest that rivets the entire country and generates a TV rating that makes Madison Avenue swoon, it is interesting to reflect back to 1967 and the modest game and innocent prelude that started it all.

Super Bowl 1 didn't have the glitz. It only had the passion, not to mention a certain mystery and mystique, that none of the 29 following events have come close to matching.

So what if a ticket cost $15 instead of the $350 gouge of a price they're charging here this year? So what if most of the country could only get casually interested, and on a warm, January, Chamber of Commerce kind of day, the Los Angeles Coliseum would only attract a crowd of 61,946?

You had to understand what this game was. And what it meant to the sport. Kansas City running back Curtis McClinton apparently did. After his Chiefs were beaten by Green Bay that day, here is what he had to say:

"I felt like one of the losers at Pompeii. . . . It was like being on a deathbed. Everything you've accomplished up to that point didn't mean a damn thing."

Football's Merger

Why did the game seem that overwhelming? Well, the older, established NFL had merged with the young, fledgling American Football League the previous October when an antitrust exemption was added as a rider to an anti-inflation tax bill President Lyndon Johnson had signed into law. It was the last legal hurdle, clearing the way for football's first "AFL-NFL World Championship Game."

The Super Bowl, as it would soon come to be known, had been born.

For some NFL players, this was just a chance for another fat postseason paycheck. For most AFL players, this was more like Armageddon. It was an opportunity for the scruffy league that had scraped and survived to finally prove it belonged with the big boys. And that feeling permeated through not only the locker rooms and front offices, but all the way to the press boxes across America.

"Objectivity went out the window when it came to this game," said Buffalo News columnist and sports editor Larry Felser, who covered the Bills and the AFL from the beginning. "The old NFL beat guys, most of whom were really third-string baseball writers, I might add, they looked at us as if we were a bunch of young punks."

Jerry Magee, who covered the Chargers back then for the *San Diego Union*, remembered when it felt like.

"To us, it was like a crusade," Magee said. "You couldn't be involved with the AFL and not feel it. We were the little guys tilting against the mighty monolith that was the NFL."

There was no media horde in Super Bowl 1. Only a collection of about 35 writers who had flown in the week before the game. . . .

A Different Game

Super Bowl 1 was just a little different.

"I can remember the Packers were staying out in Santa Barbara," Magee said. "And a colleague and I went out to their hotel. We went up to Bart Starr's room and knocked on his door. Starr opened it, saw who we were and said, 'Hey, come on in, fellas. What can I do for you?'"

In Long Beach, Hank Stram, the coach of the Chiefs, was his usual effervescent self.

"Stram was great with the press," Felser said. "I think he knew the first name of every writer who was there."

Of course, Kansas City felt it had to try harder. The Chiefs were the upstarts. The Packers, and their intimidating figure of a coach, were the legends.

"It was the first glimpse I'd had of Vince Lombardi in person," Magee said. "I remember thinking that I couldn't believe how sarcastic he was, especially with his players."

These days, the commissioner's pregame party is the event of the week, a nice, cozy gathering of 5,000 people, complete with lavish food and high-profile entertainment that costs as much as $250,000 to stage.

Back in 1967, the pregame party wasn't quite up to that.

"They had it in this small room at the hotel," Felser said, "with Les Brown and his Band of Renown. That was it."

And yet, among the athletes, the emotional buildup to this game was excruciating. The Packers felt they had to defend the honor of the NFL. As for the Chiefs . . . well, they might have taken it even more seriously.

"I was at Long Beach the morning of the game," Magee said,

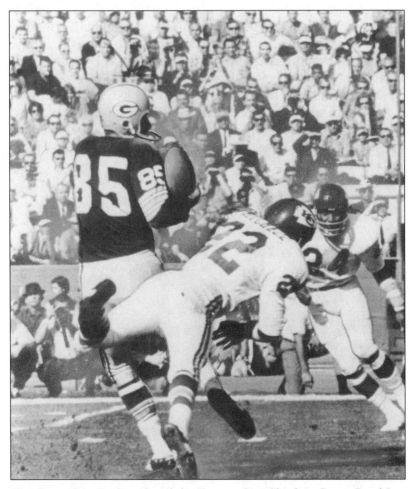

The Green Bay Packers faced the Kansas City Chiefs in Super Bowl I on January 15, 1967. The Packers beat the Chiefs 35-10.

"and it was all foggy and cold. And as I watched the Kansas City players kissing their wives and hugging their friends before getting on the bus, I swear, it looked like they were going off to war."

An Amazing Day

In a way, they were. The Chiefs had some good players, led by quarterback Len Dawson and rookie running back Mike Garrett, the Heisman Trophy winner from USC. But the Pack had Starr and Paul Hornung and Ray Nitschke and Jerry Kramer.

"The game was close for a half," Felser said, "and the old NFL guys in the press box, they were plenty nervous."

But Stram's guys couldn't match up with Lombardi's legion. The Packers buried the underdogs in the second half, winning, 35-10. And in the Green Bay locker room, it was as if a huge weight had been lifted off the team's, and the NFL's, shoulders.

"Looking back, it was truly an amazing day," Magee said. "To me, there will never be another Super Bowl like it."

And there won't be. Now there are just the jets and the limos, the hustlers and the scalpers, the overhyped week and overvalued tickets. Those who were there in 1967 can only look back and smile.

No, Super Bowl 1 wasn't necessarily bigger. Only better.

Eugene McCarthy Announces His Presidential Candidacy

By Lewis L. Gould

As the presidential election of 1968 approached, the Democratic Party faced an uncertain future. The unpopular Vietnam War and the failed Great Society of President Lyndon Johnson had taken their toll on the party. When President Johnson announced his decision to forgo the election, the Democrats scrambled to find a viable challenger for Richard Nixon. In his book *1968: The Election That Changed America*, Lewis L. Gould recounts the bleak prospects for liberals:

> Between 1964 and 1968 the Democratic party lost ground. A number of elements accounted for this political decline. The presidential leadership of Lyndon B. Johnson alienated many voters who recoiled from the Great Society's domestic programs, the Democrats' racial liberalism, and the impact of the war in Vietnam. Within four years after Johnson's smashing triumph over Barry Goldwater and the Republicans in 1964, Democrats were beleaguered and discredited. Late in 1967 Postmaster General Lawrence F. O'Brien surveyed the condition of his party and reported to President Johnson, "The Democratic party, to a greater or lesser extent, has lost contact with the voters."

The issue that attracted the most attention during the campaign leading up to the election of 1968 was the Vietnam War. In February of 1967, Senator Eugene McCarthy of Minnesota announced that he was entering the race for the Democratic nomination. McCarthy was brash and confident, and he characterized the war in Vietnam as unjust and immoral, which led to his being labeled the "antiwar" candidate. Eventually Robert Kennedy entered the fray, gaining some support from antiwar advocates. But for the early stages of the nomination process (as well as the latter stages, after Robert Kennedy's assassination) McCarthy had the support of many of liberals opposing the war. McCarthy would lose the election to Nixon despite his backing.

In the following excerpt from *1968: The Election That Changed America*, Lewis L. Gould highlights McCarthy's announcement to run and strategy as the nomination process unfolded.

L yndon Johnson's presidential decisions had propelled the United States into the major combat phase of the war in Vietnam, and it became his major political problem. If he took credit for the legislative accomplishments of his administration in domestic affairs, he could not evade responsibility for the Vietnam War that had become a foreign policy failure by late 1967.

Johnson had asked Congress for authority to make bombing strikes after North Vietnamese naval vessels allegedly attacked American ships in the Gulf of Tonkin in 1964. He had decided to bomb North Vietnam on a sustained basis in early 1965, and later that year had sent large contingents of combat troops to South Vietnam. To most of the American public, the war, whatever its origins, had become "Lyndon Johnson's War."

The president had been unable to offer a convincing rationale for U.S. involvement in this Asian conflict. He had also failed to provide a clear statement of how Americans would know when victory had been achieved. These political troubles grew out of the confused purposes within the Johnson administration itself. There the war in Vietnam was seen as part of a larger confrontation between an expansionist Communist campaign, masterminded by the Soviet Union and Communist China and working through the North Vietnamese, and the forces of Western democracy seeking to preserve the independence of South Vietnam. At the same time Washington recognized that South Vietnam lacked the internal cohesion and national will to defeat its enemy. The United States aimed to overcome this political weakness through the use of its military power until South Vietnam could stand on its own. Many observers believed that the American presence undermined a faint South Vietnamese nationalism and defeated the very goal it sought to achieve. The United States was thus trying to defend a country that seemed to lack the resolve to defend itself. . . .

McCarthy Announces Candidacy

So striking were Lyndon Johnson's political problems in late 1967 that he faced the unusual situation for an incumbent president of an important challenge to his renomination. By December 1967 Johnson had a declared opponent in the field against him and another potential rival of even greater political significance. The announced contender was Senator Eugene J. McCarthy of Minnesota, who had become a candidate on November 30. He said he would enter several primaries in order to "challenge the President's position" on Vietnam, and he argued that his campaign did not represent "any great threat to the unity and strength of the Democratic party." The other possible rival was Senator Robert F. Kennedy of New York, brother of the late president. In the later months of 1967 Kennedy had been seriously weighing a race against the president but had decided not to make the run under the existing circumstances.

When McCarthy announced, the political consensus was that he posed no serious threat to Lyndon Johnson's renomination in 1968. How could a relatively obscure senator from the upper Midwest defeat an incumbent president for renomination? When the McCarthy campaign got off to a slow start, that conventional wisdom was reinforced. By mid-December 1967 a White House aide informed the president with amusement that "Eugene McCarthy is doing so badly that I am tempted to float a rumor that he is actually working for you to dispirit the 'peace movement.'" Reports from around the country supported a discounting of McCarthy's campaign.

In fact, the McCarthy revolt against the president represented a more important political threat than the White House realized. Throughout the early months of 1968 most political observers underestimated McCarthy's capacity as a candidate. This misjudgment grew out of his mixed record as a senator since 1958. Fifty-two years old in 1968, McCarthy had won election to the

House of Representatives in 1950 and served four terms. In 1958 he ran against a popular Republican for the Senate and won a large victory in the Democratic landslide that year. He was an effective liberal legislator in his first term. His talents led Johnson to consider him closely as a vice-presidential possibility in 1964; as a liberal and a Catholic, McCarthy would have balanced the ticket well. In the end, Johnson decided that Hubert Humphrey had even better claims on the position because of his liberal accomplishments and standing within the Democratic party. The process by which Johnson led McCarthy on and then dumped him in favor of Humphrey left some scars with the senator who was a proud, even conceited, figure. Surveying the possible Democratic candidates in 1960, for example, McCarthy had quipped, "Why don't they just nominate me? I'm twice as liberal as Humphrey, twice as Catholic as Kennedy and twice as smart as [Stuart] Symington." For a man of McCarthy's self-esteem, to be turned down in favor of his Minnesota colleague whom he regarded as inferior was a wound that smarted for years. "He really felt he was led down the primrose path," a relative later recalled.

The Peace Candidate

McCarthy's willingness to challenge Johnson in 1968 did not rest simply on a personality conflict with the president. It also arose from McCarthy's reservations about the wisdom of the administration's Vietnam policy and the view of the presidency that Johnson advanced to support his actions. An initial break came during 1965 when the administration intervened in the Dominican Republic to put down an ostensible communist government in that Latin American country. By January 1966 McCarthy was also attacking the Vietnam War. So serious was the commitment of American military power, he said, that it required "a national debate, a national discussion, and a real searching of the mind and soul of America." He did not move to outright opposition to the president until 1967. On February 1 he told an audience at a peace mobilization in Washington that in the absence of positive reasons for supporting the conflict "we must be prepared to pass harsh and severe judgment on our position in this war." Four weeks later he called the war "morally unjustifiable."

Several elements led McCarthy to this position. His daughter Mary was a convinced opponent of the fighting, and she had a strong influence on her father's thinking in 1966 and 1967. The actions of the Johnson administration, and its constitutional rationale for the war, also troubled the Minnesota senator. He doubted the argument that China needed to be contained, and it bothered him when the Gulf of Tonkin resolution of 1964 was invoked to justify the president's policy. After Undersecretary of State Nicholas Katzenbach called the resolution the "functional equivalent" of a declaration of war, an angry McCarthy told a reporter, "There is no limit to what he says the president can do. There is only one thing to do—take it to the country." A suspicion of imperial presidents and their actions would be a significant theme in McCarthy's campaign in 1968.

By early 1967 McCarthy was beginning to think about mounting a challenge to Johnson, if only to provoke a debate on the wisdom of the Vietnam policy. The most formidable obstacle to such a move was Senator Robert F. Kennedy of New York, the heir apparent to his brother's political legacy. If Kennedy decided to run against Johnson, McCarthy's chances would disappear. During the autumn of 1967, however, it seemed that Kennedy was reluctant to go up against an incumbent president, and opponents of Johnson turned to other alternatives. McCarthy's possible candidacy took on new allure. . . .

Raising the Flag

In mid-October [Allard K.] Lowenstein [who spearheaded the search for an antiwar candidate] went to see McCarthy and found to his surprise that the senator was willing. "Somebody has to raise the flag," McCarthy remarked. Six days later, in a meeting with Lowenstein and another liberal leader, McCarthy made his decision definite. "You guys have been talking about three or four names. I think you can cut the list down to one now."

McCarthy proved to be a formidable candidate, but he did not seem so at first. His second term had not been a distinguished one in the Senate, in part because he had become bored with the routine of the place. His voting record on several issues revealed vulnerabilities that his opponents would exploit during 1968. He had supported the oil depletion allowance that favored the oil industry; his civil rights record was solid but seemed to lack the emotional sympathy that Robert Kennedy now displayed on this issue. He wanted to run for president in his own way and on his own terms. The McCarthy campaign was always disorganized and confused, and in his formal speeches the candidate rarely stirred his listeners.

On the other hand, McCarthy's understated style was highly congenial to the group within the Democratic party that remembered with affection the campaigns of Adlai Stevenson. There was about McCarthy much that appealed to the liberals in the suburbs who expected candidates to make rational arguments on serious issues. His laconic wit also evoked memories of John Kennedy's personal style. The senator drew on the support of independents and some Republicans who responded to his wry, literate speeches and his detached, ironic approach to political life. He was uncomfortable asking for the votes of Americans on the basis of ethnic affiliation or economic position. His constituency, he said, was "a constituency of conscience."

McCarthy intended to run in four primaries—Massachusetts, Wisconsin, Oregon, and California, states where his antiwar message would have the greatest electoral appeal. Supporters urged him also to run in the New Hampshire primary on March 12, 1968, but throughout December 1967 the senator weighed the wisdom of such a move. On January 3 he announced he would enter the New Hampshire contest. The chairman of the Democratic National Committee warned the White House that the McCarthy forces would pose a real threat to the president in both Massachusetts and New Hampshire.

Ali's Controversial Stand

By Edwin Shrake

Boxer and political activist Muhammad Ali is one of the most celebrated athletes of all time. Born Cassius Clay in Louisville, Kentucky,
on January 17, 1942, Ali quickly ascended to greatness in the boxing
ring, winning an Olympic gold medal. At the age of twenty-two, after
upsetting heavyweight champion Sonny Liston, Ali proclaimed, "I am
the greatest."

Ali was at the apex of his career in 1967, reigning as undisputed
heavyweight champion of the world. Well noted for his personality,
wit, and public persona outside the ring, Ali was extremely vocal in the
political arena. After being drafted to serve in Vietnam, Ali cited his
Muslim faith and refused to be inducted into the U.S. Army. This decision reflected growing unrest against pursuing the war in Vietnam and
gave hope to other young Americans who refused to serve.

Journalist Edwin Shrake was present in Houston in late April as Ali
faced his fateful decision with characteristic confidence. Shrake re-
counted the event in *Sports Illustrated*, his piece capturing the drama
and uncertainty of the days surrounding Ali's face-off with the U.S.
government.

For his defiance, Ali was stripped of his heavyweight title and was
prohibited from boxing publicly. Ali would return to the sport in three
years, but he never recovered the physical quickness that made him
famous.

As he looked at himself in the mirror behind the coffee-shop counter at the Hotel America in Houston early last Friday, on perhaps his final morning as heavyweight champion, Muhammad Ali was wondering how history would reflect upon him. The idea that he is an historical figure, a leader of his people, a Muslim Davy Crockett, had become an obsession and a consolation to Ali as the time approached for him to refuse to be inducted into the armed forces of the United States.

"Serious About My Religion"

Three days earlier, at lunch in another hotel, he had said, "I've left the sports pages. I've gone onto the front pages. I want to know what is right, what'll look good in history. I'm being tested by Allah. I'm giving up my title, my wealth, maybe my future. Many great men have been tested for their religious belief. If I pass this test, I'll come out stronger than ever. I've got no jails, no power, no government, but 600 million Muslims are giving me strength. Will they make me the leader of a country? Will they give me gold? Will the Supreme Being knock down the jails with an earthquake, like He could if He want? Am I a fool to give up my wealth and my title and go lay in prison? Am I a fool to give up good steaks? Do you think I'm serious? If I am, then why can't I worship as I want to in America? All I want is justice. Will I have to get that from history?"

Now, as he poked a fork at four soft-boiled egs and drank a tall glass of orange juice and a cup of coffee. Muhammad Ali—or Cassius M. Clay Jr., as it says on the legal documents that his lawyers carry into court in two cardboard boxes—was being moved by the clock toward his most fateful encounter since the night in 1964 when he knocked out Sonny Liston in Miami Beach. That one got him the heavyweight championship, and this one could lose it for him. "But not in the eyes of the people," he said. "The people know the only way I can lose my title is in the ring. My title goes where I go. But if they won't let me fight, it could cost me $10 million in earnings. Does that sound like I'm serious about my religion?"

"Come on, Champ, come on," said his New York attorney, Hayden Covington. "We've got 25 minutes."

"If we're one minute late, they're liable to shove you behind bars," his Houston attorney, Quinnan Hodges, said.

"All right, man, all right," said Ali. "If you want to go, let's go.". . .

A Soldier's Perspective

At the induction center there was a crowd of reporters and photographers but only a few curious spectators standing on the steps and on the broad walk that led into the building. Ali got out of his cab shortly before 8 A.M. When the lights of the television cameras went on, Ali shoved [friend] Bundini [Brown] away from him. Although he is largely in sympathy with the Muslims, Bundini is not a convert and they did not want his face appearing at the champion's shoulder. Ali pushed through the crowd, paused on the steps to smile for the cameras and entered an elevator in the lobby. There was such a crush of people that many of the 26 preinduction examinees [PIEs] who were reporting that morning [April 28] for Houston's Board No. 61 could not get on the elevator, causing the examination schedule to begin 15 minutes late. One of the PIEs, John McCulloch, 22, of Sam Houston State College, was forced back against the wall by the wake of the champion's following. Clutching his canvas overnight bag—an item Ali did not bother to bring, since he knew he would not be leaving on the 6 P.M. bus for Fort Polk, La.—McCulloch said, "I feel kind of sorry for the old guy. He can't get away from all this mess."

On the third floor Ali was taken down the hall past a barrier guarded by soldiers. After roll call he began his physical examination. A mental examination was not required, because the results of Ali's previous mental exam were available to the processing personnel. "It was great, the way he came in," said Ron Holland, a PIE transfer from Escondido, Calif. "'You all look very dejected,' he told us. 'I'm gonna tell you some jokes.' He was very cheerful. He cheered us all up. He talked about Floyd Patterson. I asked him about that Russian who is supposed to be such a good boxer, and he said, 'We'll take care of him.' He told us his mind was made up. He said if he went into the Army and the Viet Cong didn't get him, some red-neck from Georgia would. He was in good spirits. I got his autograph. I've been in this examining center before, and this was the first time I've been treated so well. I think the Army was trying to impress the champ. He even told me to hang around and he'd see that I got out of the building all right in case there was a riot or something outside."

Preparing for the Event

Ali had been preparing for weeks for the moment when he would refuse to take the symbolic one step forward that would put him into the service. He had decided at least two weeks earlier on his course of action.

The refusal to take that one step forward, Ali had been told, was the only way he could get his case judged in court in a civil suit. In any controversy with the government, a citizen must, in legal terms, "exhaust his administrative remedies" before he can be heard in a civil proceeding by a federal judge. Ali's request for a draft exemption on the grounds that he is a Muslim minister had been denied not in court but by the Selective Service Board of Kentucky, by National Selective Service System Director Lieut. General Lewis Hershey and by Judge Henry Gwiazda, Dr. Kenneth W. Clement and Commissioner Charles Collatos, members of the three-man National Selective Service Appeal Board. Until Ali actually showed up for induction and refused to take the one step forward that is, in effect, an oath, his administrative remedies were not exhausted—which explains why there had been so many appeals, requests and suits filed by Covington and Hodges. . . .

"We Don't Want Violence"

Ali returned to Houston from a trip to Chicago, Louisville and Washington, on the Monday night of his final week before reporting for induction. Covington and Hodges met him at the airport. He got into the back seat of a white convertible and asked to be driven to his apartment. "This won't blow my hair, will it?" he asked laughing. "Hey, lawyers, I been in jail. I went to a jail in Washington, just checking the place out, you know. They live nice in that jail. They got a gym, TV, good food. The prisoners heard I was there and the warden asked me to speak before they tore up the place. Then I went into the streets and spoke to thousands. I signed autographs for two and a half hours. I got thousands coming to the faith. What does it take to make me a minister? Why they want to put a man like me in the Army? If I have to die, I'll die. Most people die for nothing. I'll at least be dying for something."

Cruising along through the warm, blue Houston night, Ali directed the driver to stop at a bowling alley. "I'll show you what the people think of me," he said. Inside were a few whites and about 50 Negroes. Ali walked among them, kissing babies, shaking hands, always looking over his shoulders to see who was coming up next. Rather disappointed with his reception, he went back to the car and was driven to Texas Southern University where roughly 100 Negro students had gathered on the sidewalk, not knowing they were to be visited. More than a week before, they had been throwing bottles and bricks through car windshields in a protest inspired by Stokely Carmichael. This evening Ali jumped out of his car, threw up his arms and shouted, "I'm ready to rumble."

"Hi, soul," somebody yelled. "Hi, brother," shouted Ali.

The students gathered around him, while Hodges and Covington waited in the car.

"Burn their babies," a student said.

"Stokely, he tell the word to burn Whitey," said another.

"I'm telling you religion," Ali said.

"Naw, not religion. We want to burn Whitey."

"Don't do nothing violent. We're not violent," said the champion.

"This is rebellion, man. They take you in the Army, they see a rebellion."

"Stokely say burn their babies."

"We don't want violence," Ali said.

"You don't put down a black brother," said a little guy with a mustache.

"Are you married?" Ali asked a girl.

"Yeah, man. I'm married to SNCC [Student Nonviolent Coordinating Committee]," she answered.

After a few more minutes of listening to shouted slogans, Ali returned to the car. "They're a bunch of young fools," he said. "I don't want any of this violence. I hear there'll be demonstrations Friday morning in New York, Chicago, London, Egypt. There are 16,000 Muslims in Cleveland who'll demonstrate. Jim Brown's organization called me about that. Muslims are flying in from all over the country. Nearly every Negro is a Muslim at heart. The trouble is, first thing you got to do to be a Muslim is live a righteous life. Most people, white or black don't want to do that.". . .

Testifying

At noon the next day Ali went to lunch at the exclusive Houston Club with Hodges, Covington, U.S. Attorney Morton Susman, Assistant U.S. Attorney Carl Walker and a local Muslim minister, Raymond X (né Watlington). Susman, a Jew, and Walker, a

Negro, were to take the government side in Ali's final pre-induction appeal, with two native white Texans defending Ali, an irony that was duly remarked upon. While the lawyers discussed ground rules, Ali launched into a typical speech about his religion.

"Blacks and whites are dying in Vietnam so those people over there will have the freedom to worship as they want," he said. "So how come I can't do it here?" He is not necessarily opposed to the war in Vietnam, merely to his own presence in the armed services. . . .

The champion went to the airport and flew to Chicago to close up his suite at a motel, put his Cadillac into a garage and deposit some money in his bank. While in Chicago he discussed the house he wants to buy. It would have a Muhammad Ali museum in the basement and a movie screen to show his fights to his grandchildren. . . .

Ali returned to Houston and met with Covington and Hodges for lunch at the Rice Hotel on Thursday. . . .

They were on their way to the Federal District Court of Judge Allen Hannay. Covington and Hodges were seeking a restraining order to prevent the Selective Service boards of Kentucky and Texas, as well as General Hershey, from reporting Ali as delinquent until his request for an exemption could be ruled on in federal court as a civil matter. Under normal procedure, when Ali refused to take the one step forward, he was to be reported as delinquent, which could result in a criminal charge. Eventually he would be indicted and arrested. That was what Ali's attorneys wished to avoid. . . .

Judge Hannay, who had the lined red face and brief smile of an old cowboy, an appearance he got by playing golf frequently at Houston's River Oaks Country Club, seemed very interested in having Ali in his witness box. In the hall Ali had told some Texas Southern students who spoke of protest, "I don't want you suffering just because I suffer. Don't get hurt. They're talking about filling the jails." To Judge Hannay, Ali was courteous, always saying, "sir." But his testimony made the judge blink.

Ali told how he had been approached by the Muslims in Miami in 1961 and had finally been sold on the religion shortly before the Liston fight in 1964. He said "Old McDonald" (Promoter Bill McDonald) had tried to make him renounce his religion but he had refused. He claimed that he had packed his bags and climbed aboard a bus to leave Miami Beach, even though he owed $64,000, before McDonald relented.

After that demonstration of his sincerity, Ali testified, he was given the Muslim name of Muhammad Ali—meaning "one who is worthy of praise"—which was recorded in the Muslims' Lamb's Book of Life. Ali then became a minister of his religion, one that is known as the Lost Found Nation of Islam in North America. . . .

About serving in the armed forces, he said: "It's against the teachings of the Holy Koran. I'm not trying to dodge the draft. We are not supposed to take part in no wars unless declared by Allah or by The Messenger [Elijah Muhammad]. Muhammad was a warrior 1,400 years ago but he was a holy warrior fighting in the name of Allah. We don't take part in Christian wars or wars of any unbelievers. We aren't Christian or Communist."

Fascinated, the judge bent forward and asked, "In a conflict between Communism and Christianity, which side would you take?"

"Neither side, Judge," replied Ali.

After Bundini Brown had testified to Ali's sincerity, the cham-

Muhammad Ali leaves the U.S. Army induction center in Houston. Ali lost his heavyweight title when he refused to serve in the armed forces.

pion's party loaded into an airport limousine, went to Hodges' office and then began a customary romp through the streets. . . .

Protests at the Induction Center

The next morning, while Ali was closed off in the examining room at the induction station, three or four whites who had come down from Long Island to work at an Indian reservation in Oklahoma were protesting out front with 11 Negroes, several dressed up in African suits made out of sheets and sandals. It was hardly the mass protest Ali had predicted.

The photographers and reporters, who outnumbered the protesters 10 to 1, immediately demonstrated one basic flaw in modern journalism. They photographed and interviewed all the protesters, thus giving weight to what was a very puny demonstration by—except for one cute girl—a very scraggly-looking bunch. There have been few demonstrations or protests of any sort in Houston—a fact the city is smugly proud of and one that could change suddenly and explosively this summer. "We integrated this city quietly, without any fuss, by agreement, and we have no trouble" is what one hears in Houston. . . .

In front of the induction center five Negro students were burning their draft cards while a score of others, coming in at noon, marched in a circle carrying placards and a Black Power flag. They sang songs about black nationalism. They chanted, "Keep the faith." They read from the writings of Malcolm X—"Whoever heard of a revolution where they lock arms and sing *We Shall Overcome?*" and, "America is a house on fire. Let it burn, let it burn." They shouted racist clichés: "blue-eyed devils," "send them to their graves," "Molotov cocktails," "Black Power," "Whitey's war."

Up on the steps stood G-men wearing red bands in their left lapels and carrying walkie-talkie radios. Morton Susman sat on the steps, his radio muffled in a cardboard folder, looking slightly embarrassed by the squawking. The protesters kept marching in a circle, waiting for Ali to come out, looking for a leader, Ali was inside, eating his box lunch, tossing aside the ham sandwich.

Moment of Truth

When the moment came, he refused three times to step forward at the call of his name. Navy Lieutenant C.P. Hartman called him into his office and warned him he was committing a felony punishable by five years in prison and a fine of $10,000. Ali then returned to the big room and again refused to answer his name, whereupon he was asked to write, "I refuse to be inducted into the armed forces of the United States." He signed his name, making the refusal official. Susman was notified, though he was hardly surprised. The procedure is for Lieut. Colonel J.E. Mc-Kee, commanding officer of the induction station, to notify the Selective Service Board of Texas, which notifies the Kentucky board, which notifies Hershey, who refers the matter to the Justice Department, which hands it back to Susman, who goes before a federal grand jury to request an indictment. That process will require from 30 to 60 days, in Susman's estimate. The government obviously is not anxious to rush Ali off in manacles.

Covington and Hodges have filed further legal actions. Even if a federal court rules that Ali is not a minister of the Muslim faith—which, according to Covington, has been adjudged a religion and not a sect in several decisions—and he is found guilty of violating the Universal Military Training and Service Act, it could be two years or more before Ali enters prison. But he has been prejudged, as he knew he would be, by boxing authorities. "That's what really hurts," said Hodges. "In the law, a man is innocent until he is proven guilty. Muhammad Ali has not even been charged with a crime yet, and they're all leaping in to strip him of his title."

Ali had little to say about it except for a prepared statement. He was under orders from Elijah Muhammad to keep his mouth shut. He went back to the Hotel America and called Herbert Muhammad. Then he curled up on his bed and phoned his mother in Louisville. "Mama," he said. "I'm all right. I did what I had to do. I sure am looking forward to coming home to eat some of your cooking."

Abbie Hoffman Leads Protests in Major Cities

By Abbie Hoffman

Of the legions of protestors, dissidents, and self-proclaimed revolutionaries of the 1960s, Abbie Hoffman is one of the most recognizable and influential. Articulate, intelligent, and fearless, Hoffman used his biting wit and everyman persona to help organize some of the most notable protests of the era. Chicago, San Francisco, New York, and Washington were some of the staging grounds for the often bizarre but usually effective protest events led by Hoffman.

Hoffman was an accomplished writer, and his ability to attract media attention with his unorthodox and unconventional methods of protest contributed to his appeal. He was a founding member of the Yippie Party, which staged serious protests through often farcical methods. In his 1989 book *Revolution for the Hell of It*, Hoffman gives a characteristically flippant and disjointed account of two incidents that he planned and executed in 1967, in an attempt to show how absorbed Americans were with money and war: the symbolic release of dollar bills onto the floor of the New York Stock Exchange, and the "exorcism" of the Pentagon, during which Hoffman and other notable public organizers and activists attempted to surround and levitate the building. Though seemingly inconsequential and ridiculous at the time, these incidents were followed by more traditional serious and widespread protests that began occurring around the nation, such as at the Chicago Democratic National Convention of 1968, where Hoffman was arrested as part of the group of activists protesting the war in Vietnam.

Abbie Hoffman continued a successful career as a public organizer and environmentalist until his death in 1989.

MAY 20, 1967: At first I thought throwing out money at the Stock Exchange was just a minor bit of theater. I had more important things to do, like raising bail money for a busted brother. Reluctantly, I called up and made arrangements for a tour under the name of George Metesky, Chairman of East Side Service Organization (ESSO). We didn't even bother to call the press. About eighteen of us showed up. When we went in the guards immediately confronted us. "You are hippies here to have a demonstration and we cannot allow that in the Stock Exchange." "Who's a hippie? I'm Jewish and besides we don't do demonstrations, see we have no picket signs," I shot back. The guards decided it was not a good idea to keep a Jew out of the Stock Exchange, so they agreed we could go in. We stood in line with all the other tourists, exchanging stories. When the line moved around the corner, we saw more newsmen than I've ever seen in such a small area. We started clowning. Eating money, kissing and hugging, and that sort of stuff. The newsmen were told by the guards that they could not enter the gallery with us. We were ushered in and immediately started throwing money over the railing. The big tickertape stopped and the brokers let out a mighty cheer. The guards started pushing us and the brokers booed. When we got out, I carried on in front of the press.

"Who are you?"

"I'm Cardinal Spellman."

"Where did you get the money?"

"I'm Cardinal Spellman, you don't ask me where I get my money."

"How much did you throw out?"

"A thousand dollars in small bills."

"How many of you are there?"

"Two, three, we don't even exist! We don't even exist!"

We danced in front of the Stock Exchange, celebrating the end of money. I burned a fiver. Some guy said it was disgusting and I agreed with him, calling my comrades "Filthy Commies."

The TV show that night was fantastic. It went all over the world. TV news shows always have a pattern. First the "serious" news, all made up, of course, a few commercials, often constructed better than the news, then the Stock Market Report. Then the upswing human interest story to keep everybody happy as cows. Our thing came after the Stock Market Report, it was a natural. CBS, which is the most creative network, left in references to Cardinal Spellman; I was surprised at that. Every news report differed. Some said we threw out monopoly money, some said twenty–thirty dollars, some said over $100, some said the bills were all ripped up first. It was a perfect mythical event, since every reporter, not being allowed to actually witness the scene, had to make up his own fantasy. Some had interesting fantasies, some boring. One tourist who joined the exorcism got the point: "I'm from Missouri and I've been throwing away money in New York for five days now. This is sure a hell of a lot quicker and more fun.". . .

Raising the Pentagon

SEPTEMBER 28, 1967: . . . We are throwing everything we've got at the Pentagon—evil hulk that sits like a cancerous death-trap on the beautiful Potomac. An Exorcism to cast out the evil spirits on October 21st. The Pentagon shall not survive. . . .

Many wild happenings are planned in preparation: circling of Washington Monument, Empire State Building (vertically), Make Love Day orgy leading up to October 21st [1967]. On Columbus Day a mighty caravan of wagons will roll East out of San Francisco to rediscover America complete with real live Indian scouts, compliments of Chief Rolling Thunder of the Shoshone. Junk cars, stolen buses, motorcycles, rock bands, flower banners, dope, incense, and enough food for the long journey. Wagon train East. Yahoo! We will dye the Potomac red, burn the cherry trees, panhandle embassies, attack with water pistols, marbles, bubble gum wrappers, bazookas, girls will run naked and piss on the Pentagon walls, sorcerers, swamis, witches, voodoo, warlocks, medicine men, and speed freaks will hurl their magic at the faded brown walls. Rock bands will bomb out with "Joshua fit the Battle of Jericho." We will dance and sing and chant the mighty OM. We will fuck on the grass and beat ourselves against the doors. Everyone will scream "VOTE

FOR ME." We shall raise the flag of nothingness over the Pentagon and a mighty cheer of liberation will echo through the land. "We are Free, Great God Almighty, Free at last." Schoolchildren will rip out their desks and throw ink at stunned instructors, office secretaries will disrobe and run into the streets, newsboys will rip up their newspapers and sit on the curbstones masturbating, storekeepers will throw open their doors making everything free, accountants will all collapse in one mighty heart attack, soldiers will throw down their guns. . . .

Are You Guys Serious?

The peace movement has gone crazy and it's about time. Our alternative fantasy will match in zaniness the war in Vietnam. Fantasy is Freedom. Anybody can do anything. "The Pentagon will rise 300 feet in the air."

No rules, speeches won't do, leaders are all full of shit. Pull your clothes off (MAKE LOVE, NOT WAR), punch a marshal, jump a wall, do a dance, sing a song, paint the building, blow it up, charge and get inside.

FLASHBACK: "67-68-69-70-"

"What do you think you guys are doing?"

"Measuring the Pentagon. We have to see how many people we'll need to form a ring around it."

"You're what!"

"It's very simple. You see, the Pentagon is a symbol of evil in most religions. You're religious, aren't you?"

"Unh."

"Well, the only way to exorcise the evil spirits here is to form a circle around the Pentagon. *87-88-89* . . ."

The two scouts are soon surrounded by a corps of guards, FBI agents, soldiers and some mighty impressive brass.

"*112-113-114-*"

"Are you guys serious? It's against the law to measure the Pentagon."

"Are you guys serious? Show us the law. *237-238-239-240.* That does it. Colonel, how much is *240* times *5?*"

"What? What the hell's going on here!"

"*1200*," answers Bruce, an impressive-looking agent who tells us later he works in a security department that doesn't even have a name yet.

We show them our exorcism flyers. They bust us for littering.

"Shades of Alice's Restaurant. Are you guys kidding? That ain't litter, it's art."

"Litter."

"Art."

"Litter."

"How about Litter Art?" says Bruce after two hours.

We are free to go, but have to be very sneaky and ditch Bruce somewhere inside the Pentagon maze so he won't find the Acapulco Gold [drugs] in the car.

The magic is beginning to work, but the media must be convinced. You simply cannot call them up and say, "Pardon me, but the Pentagon will rise in the air on October 21st." You've got to show them.

Friday, the 13th, Village Theater, warlocks, witches, speed freaks, Fugs and assorted kooks plus one non-believer named Krassner. "Out, Demons, Out!"—and, *zip*, up goes the mock Pentagon. "Higher! Higher! Higher!"

(Is it legal to cry *Higher* in a crowded theater?)

We burn the model and will use its ashes on Big Daddy the following week. Media is free. Use it. Don't pay for it. Don't buy ads. Make news. . . .

The Pentagon happening transcended the issue of the War. "*The War Is Over*," sings Phil Ochs, and the protest becomes directed to the entire fabric of a restrictive, dull, brutal society.

The protesters become total political animals.

A totality emerges that renders the word *political* meaningless. "The war is over." Everybody's yelling and screaming. Someone writes LBJ LOVES HO CHI MINH on the wall.

> Ring around the Pentagon, a pocket full of pot
> Four and twenty generals all begin to rot.
> All the evil spirits start to tumble out
> Now the war is over, we all begin to shout.

The soldiers have a choice. "Join us! Join us!"—the cry goes up. Three do. Drop their helmets and guns and break ranks. They are caught by the marshals and dragged away into oblivion and the third degree. . . .

The Battle Is Over

Sunday at the Pentagon is a different scene. A mind trip working on the troops. Ex-soldiers talk to MPs. So do girls, college kids and priests for twelve long hours. Talking, singing, sharing, contrasting Free America vs. the Uniformed Machine. At midnight the Pentagon speaks after two days of silence.

"Your permit has expired. If you do not leave the area you will be arrested. All demonstrators are requested to leave the area at once. This is a recorded announcement."

"Fuck you, Pentagon. I'm not a demonstrator. I'm a tourist."

Everybody is herded into vans. The door slams shut but the lock doesn't work.

"The New Action Army sure is a pisser."

The MPs laugh and finally get the bolt in place. Off we go to Occoquan and jail land. "Carry me back to Ol' Virginny . . ." I hate jail. I try to chew my way through the van door and am doing pretty well when some of the girls get scared. . . .

Jail is a goof. Easiest jailing of all time. The Army is into brainwashing. Clean sheets, good breakfast, propaganda radio station.

We call the guard and demand to be treated as prisoners of war. He listens patiently as we ask for the International Red Cross and other courtesies accorded under the Geneva Convention. He scratches his head and walks away. . . .

Everybody's making the sign of the V. The battle is over. The question everyone's asking is when's the next happening?

The Black Panthers Prophesy Another Revolution

By Huey P. Newton

The Black Panther Party burst into national consciousness on May 2, 1967, when party cofounder Huey P. Newton delivered a rousing anti-government statement at the California State Capitol building. Newton and his compatriots urged African Americans to join a new, proactive, and sometimes-violent movement to achieve basic freedoms. Newton's professed methods were in stark contrast to the nonviolent approach promoted by Reverend Martin Luther King Jr. Newton believed that only by showing strength would African Americans undo oppression. Armed with rifles and other weapons (which were legal to carry on the streets), Newton, Bobby Seale, and other party members struck a discordant pose in front of mainstream America, in a precursor to the vicious summer riots that would tear apart numerous cities in 1967.

Soon the militant politics and methods of the Black Panthers were etched into the mind of a nation undergoing growing pains and erasing decades of segregation. Full of internal struggles and facing the external pressures of a fearful public, the Panthers nonetheless became, for a short time, one of the most influential political organizations of the turbulent 1960s.

The following are excerpts from two speeches Huey Newton gave in 1967, in which he gives his own interpretation of the struggles and ob-

Huey P. Newton, *To Die for the People: The Writings of Huey P. Newton*. New York: Random House, 1972. Copyright © 1972 by Stronghold Consolidated Productions. All rights reserved. Reproduced by permission of Random House, Inc., and Lubell, Lubell, Fine & Schaap.

stacles facing African Americans at that time. The first speech, from June 20, provides Newton's argument on how an armed rebellion among blacks will bring down the white racist regime that not only oppresses its own citizens but also powerless people in other nations. In the second speech, given on July 20, Newton defines how the Black Panther Party must educate the oppressed masses and lead them through the stages of a successful revolution in America.

I

Men were not created in order to obey laws. Laws are created to obey men. They are established by men and should serve men. The laws and rules which officials inflict upon poor people prevent them from functioning harmoniously in society. There is no disagreement about this function of law in any circle—the disagreement arises from the question of which men laws are to serve. Such lawmakers ignore the fact that it is the duty of the poor and unrepresented to construct rules and laws that serve their interests better. Rewriting unjust laws is a basic human right and fundamental obligation.

Abolishing the System

Before 1776 America was a British colony. The British Government had certain laws and rules that the colonized Americans rejected as not being in their best interests. In spite of the British conviction that Americans had no right to establish their own laws to promote the general welfare of the people living here in America, the colonized immigrant felt he had no choice but to raise the gun to defend his welfare. Simultaneously he made certain laws to ensure his protection from external and internal aggressions, from other governments, and his own agencies. One such form of protection was the Declaration of Independence, which states: ". . . whenever any government becomes destructive to these ends, it is the right of the people to alter or to abolish it, and to institute a new government, laying its foundations on such principles and organizing its powers in such forms as to them shall seem most likely to effect their safety and happiness."

Now these same colonized White people, these bondsmen, paupers, and thieves deny the colonized Black man not only the right to abolish this oppressive system, but to even *speak* of abolishing it. Having carried this madness and cruelty to the four corners of the earth, there is now universal rebellion against their continued rule and power. But as long as the wheels of the imperialistic war machine are turning, there is no country that can defeat this monster of the West. It is our belief that the Black people in America are the only people who can free the world, loosen the yoke of colonialism, and destroy the war machine. Black people who are within the machine can cause it to malfunction. They can, because of their intimacy with the mechanism, destroy the engine that is enslaving the world. America will not be able to fight every Black country in the world and fight a civil war at the same time. It is militarily impossible to do both of these things at once.

Speedy Liberation

The slavery of Blacks in this country provides the oil for the machinery of war that America uses to enslave the peoples of the world. Without this oil the machinery cannot function. We are the driving shaft; we are in such a strategic position in this machinery that, once we become dislocated, the functioning of the remainder of the machinery breaks down.

Penned up in the ghettos of America, surrounded by his factories and all the physical components of his economic system, we have been made into "the wretched of the earth," relegated to the position of spectators while the White racists run their international con game on the suffering peoples. We have been brainwashed to believe that we are powerless and that there is nothing we can do for ourselves to bring about a speedy liberation for our people. We have been taught that we must please our oppressors, that we are only ten percent of the population, and therefore must confine our tactics to categories calculated not to disturb the sleep of our tormentors.

The power structure inflicts pain and brutality upon the peoples and then provides controlled outlets for the pain in ways least likely to upset them, or interfere with the process of exploitation. The people must repudiate the established channels as tricks and deceitful snares of the exploiting oppressors. The people must oppose everything the oppressor supports, and support everything that he opposes. If Black people go about their struggle for liberation in the way that the oppressor dictates and sponsors, then we will have degenerated to the level of groveling flunkies for the oppressor himself. When the oppressor makes a vicious attack against freedom-fighters because of the

way that such freedom-fighters choose to go about their liberation, then we know we are moving in the direction of our liberation. The racist dog oppressors have no rights which oppressed
Black people are bound to respect. As long as the racist dogs pol-
lute the earth with the evil of their actions, they do not deserve
any respect at all, and the "rules" of their game, written in the
people's blood, are beneath contempt.

Organized Power

The oppressor must be harassed until his doom. He must have
no peace by day or by night. The slaves have always outnumbered the slavemasters. The power of the oppressor rests upon
the submission of the people. When Black people really unite
and rise up in all their splendid millions, they will have the
strength to smash injustice. We do not understand the power in
our numbers. We are millions and millions of Black people scat-
tered across the continent and throughout the Western Hemi-
sphere. There are more Black people in America than the total
population of many countries now enjoying full membership in
the United Nations. They have power and their power is based
primarily on the fact that they are organized and united with each
other. They are recognized by the powers of the world.

We, with all our numbers, are recognized by no one. In fact,
we do not even recognize our own selves. We are unaware of the
potential power latent in our numbers. In 1967, in the midst of a
hostile racist nation whose hidden racism is rising to the surface
at a phenomenal speed, we are still so blind to our critical fight
for our very survival that we are continuing to function in petty,
futile ways. Divided, confused, fighting among ourselves, we are
still in the elementary stage of throwing rocks, sticks, empty
wine bottles and beer cans at racist police who lie in wait for a
chance to murder unarmed Black people. The racist police have
worked out a system for suppressing these spontaneous rebellions that flare up from the anger, frustration, and desperation of
the masses of Black people. We can no longer afford the dubious luxury of the terrible casualties wantonly inflicted upon us
by the police during these rebellions.

By Any Means Necessary

Black people must now move, from the grass roots up through
the perfumed circles of the Black bourgeoisie, to seize by any

means necessary a proportionate share of the power vested and collected in the structure of America. We must organize and unite to combat by long resistance the brutal force used against us daily. The power structure depends upon the use of force within retaliation. This is why they have made it a felony to teach guerrilla warfare. This is why they want the people unarmed.

The racist dog oppressors fear the armed people; they fear most of all Black people armed with weapons and the ideology of the Black Panther Party for Self-Defense. An unarmed people are slaves or are subject to slavery at any given moment. If a government is not afraid of the people it will arm the people against foreign aggression. Black people are held captive in the midst of their oppressors. There is a world of difference between thirty million unarmed submissive Black people and thirty million Black people armed with freedom, guns, and the strategic methods of liberation.

When a mechanic wants to fix a broken-down car engine, he must have the necessary tools to do the job. When the people move for liberation they must have the basic tool of liberation: the gun. Only with the power of the gun can the Black masses halt the terror and brutality directed against them by the armed racist power structure; and in one sense only by the power of the gun can the whole world be transformed into the earthly paradise dreamed of by the people from time immemorial. One successful practitioner of the art and science of national liberation and self-defense, Brother Mao Tse-tung, put it this way: "We are advocates of the abolition of war, we do not want war; but war can only be abolished through war, and in order to get rid of the gun it is necessary to take up the gun."

The blood, sweat, tears and suffering of Black people are the foundations of the wealth and power of the United States of America. We were forced to build America, and if forced to, we will tear it down. The immediate result of this destruction will be suffering and bloodshed. But the end result will be the perpetual peace for all mankind. . . .

II

The Black masses are handling the resistance incorrectly. When the brothers in East Oakland, having learned their resistance fighting from Watts, amassed the people in the streets, threw bricks and Molotov cocktails to destroy property and create disruption, they were herded into a small area by the gestapo police and immediately contained by the brutal violence of the oppressor's storm troops. Although this manner of resistance is sporadic, short-lived, and costly, it has been transmitted across the country to all the ghettos of the Black nation.

The identity of the first man who threw a Molotov cocktail is not known by the masses, yet they respect and imitate his action. In the same way, the actions of the party will be imitated by the people—if the people respect these activities.

The primary job of the party is to provide leadership for the people. It must teach by words and action the correct strategic methods of prolonged resistance. When the people learn that it is no longer advantageous for them to resist by going into the streets in large numbers, and when they see the advantage in the activities of the guerrilla warfare method, they will quickly follow this example.

But first, they must respect the party which is transmitting this message. When the vanguard group destroys the machinery of the oppressor by dealing with him in small groups of three and four, and then escapes the might of the oppressor, the masses will be impressed and more likely to adhere to this correct strategy. When the masses hear that a gestapo policeman has been executed while sipping coffee at a counter, and the revolutionary executioners fled without being traced, the masses will see the validity of this kind of resistance. It is not necessary to organize thirty million Black people in primary groups of two's and three's, but it is important for the party to show the people how to stage a revolution.

A Revolutionary Education

There are three ways one can learn: through study, observation, and experience. Since the Black community is composed basically of activists, observation of or participation in activity are the principle ways the community learns. To learn by studying is good, but to learn by experience is better. Because the Black community is not a reading community it is very important that the vanguard group be essentially activists. Without this knowledge of the Black community a Black revolution in racist America is impossible.

The main function of the party is to awaken the people and teach them the strategic method of resisting a power structure which is prepared not only to combat with massive brutality the people's resistance but to annihilate totally the Black population. If it is learned by the power structure that Black people have "X" number of guns in their possession, that information will not stimulate the power structure to prepare itself with guns; it is already prepared.

The end result of this revolutionary education will be positive for Black people in their resistance, and negative for the power structure in its oppression because the party always exemplifies revolutionary defiance. If the party does not make the people aware of the tools and methods of liberation, there will be no means by which the people can mobilize.

The Masses

The relationship between the vanguard party and the masses is a secondary relationship. The relationship among the members of the vanguard party is a primary relationship. If the party machinery is to be effective it is important that the members of the party group maintain a face-to-face relationship with each other. It is impossible to put together functional party machinery or programs without this direct relationship. To minimize the danger of Uncle Tom informers and opportunists the members of the vanguard group should be tested revolutionaries.

The main purpose of the vanguard group should be to raise the consciousness of the masses through educational programs and other activities. The sleeping masses must be bombarded with the correct approach to struggle and the party must use all means available to get this information across to the masses. In order to do so the masses must know that the party exists. A vanguard party is never underground in the beginning of its existence; that would limit its effectiveness and educational goals. How can you teach people if the people do not know and respect you? The party must exist aboveground as long as the dog power structure will allow, and, hopefully, when the party is forced to go underground, the party's message will already have been put across to the people. The vanguard party's activities on the surface will necessarily be short-lived. Thus the party must make a tremendous impact upon the people before it is driven into secrecy. By that time the people will know the party exists and will seek further information about its activities when it is driven underground.

Many would-be revolutionaries work under the fallacious notion that the vanguard party should be a secret organization which the power structure knows nothing about, and that the masses know nothing about except for occasional letters that come to their homes by night. Underground parties cannot distribute leaflets announcing an underground meeting. Such contradictions and inconsistencies are not recognized by these so-called revolutionaries. They are, in fact, afraid of the very danger that they are asking the people to confront. These so-called revolutionaries want the people to say what they themselves are afraid to say, to do what they themselves are afraid to do. That kind of revolutionary is a coward and a hypocrite. A true revolutionary realizes that if he is sincere death is imminent. The things he is saying and doing are extremely dangerous. Without this realization it is pointless to proceed as a revolutionary.

The History of Revolution

If these imposters would investigate the history of revolution they would see that the vanguard group always starts out aboveground and is driven underground by the aggressor. The Cuban Revolution is an example: when Fidel Castro started to resist the butcher [Cuban dictator Fulgencio] Batista and the American running dogs, he began by speaking publicly on the University of Havana campus. He was later driven to the hills. His impact upon the dispossessed people of Cuba was tremendous and his teachings were received with much respect. When he went into hiding, the Cuban people searched him out, going to the hills to find him and his band of twelve.

Castro handled the revolutionary struggle correctly, and if the Chinese Revolution is investigated it will be seen that the Communist Party operated quite openly in order to muster support from the masses. There are many more examples of successful revolutionary struggle from which one can learn the correct approach: the revolution in Kenya, the Algerian Revolution discussed in Frantz Fanon's *The Wretched of the Earth*, the Russian Revolution, the works of Chairman Mao Tse-tung, and a host of others.

Millions and millions of oppressed people may not know members of the vanguard party personally but they will learn of its activities and its proper strategy for liberation through an indirect acquaintance provided by the mass media. But it is not enough to rely on the media of the power structure; it is of prime importance that the vanguard party develop its own communications organ, such as a newspaper, and at the same time provide strategic revolutionary art, and destruction of the oppressor's machinery. For example in Watts the economy and property of the oppressor was destroyed to such an extent that no matter how the oppressor tried in his press to whitewash the activities of the Black brothers, the real nature and cause of the activity was communicated to every Black community. And no matter how the oppressor tried in his own media to distort and confuse the message of Brother Stokely Carmichael, Black people all over the country understood it perfectly and welcomed it.

Arming the Community

The Black Panther Party for Self-Defense teaches that, in the final analysis the guns, hand grenades, bazookas, and other equipment necessary for defense must be supplied by the power structure. As exemplified by the Vietcong, these weapons must be taken from the oppressor. Therefore, the greater the military preparation on the part of the oppressor, the greater the availability of weapons for the Black community. It is believed by some hypocrites that when the people are taught by the vanguard group to prepare for resistance, this only brings "the man" down on them with increasing violence and brutality; but the fact is that when the man becomes more oppressive he only heightens revolutionary fervor. So if things get worse for oppressed people they will feel the need for revolution and resistance. The people make revolution; the oppressors, by their brutal actions, cause resistance by the people. The vanguard party only teaches the correct methods of resistance.

The complaint of the hypocrites that the Black Panther Party for Self-Defense is exposing the people to deeper suffering is an incorrect observation. By their rebellions in the Black communities across the country the people have proved that they will not tolerate any more oppression by the racist dog police. They are looking now for guidance to extend and strengthen their resistance struggle. The vanguard party must exemplify the characteristics that make them worthy of leadership.

ARTICLE 6

Race Riots Shatter the Peace in Detroit

Part I: Associated Press; Part II: Jerry M. Flint; Part III: Hubert G. Locke

The summer of 1967 is often referred to as the "long, hot summer," in reference to the extremely hot weather and violent race riots that plagued the United States. Caused by a variety of factors, including racial tensions and police brutality, major outbreaks of racial violence shattered the peace in Grand Rapids, Michigan; Toledo, Ohio; Rochester, New York; and Phoenix, Arizona. On July 12, Newark, New Jersey, was rocked by extensive rioting and looting. Three weeks later the worst incident took place in Detroit, Michigan. The Detroit riots erupted on July 23 and lasted five days, resulting in unprecedented numbers of deaths, injuries, arrests, and property loss.

The city of Detroit faced a long recovery from the riots. Its infrastructure ripped apart, the city witnessed a "white flight" as many white inner-city residents moved to the suburbs. As Detroit's wealthiest citizens fled the city, the poor and disenfranchised were left to pick up the pieces.

Many reporters experienced the riots firsthand as they unfolded, braving sniper fire, police and National Guard brutality, and an out of control mob of looters and rioters. The following descriptions include Associated Press reports on the devastating second day of the riots (Part I), a *New York Times* piece by Jerry M. Flint on the final day

(Part II), as well as a reflective piece by Hubert G. Locke from his book *The Detroit Riot of 1967* in which the author discusses the lessons learned from the event (Part III).

I

Thousands of rampaging Negroes firebombed and looted huge sections of Detroit last night and early today. Gov. George Romney ordered 1,500 National Guardsmen, backed by tanks, to quell the riot.

Violence spread uncontrolled over most sections of the city. Destructive fury swept along three-mile and four-mile sections of streets crisscrossing the heart of Detroit and ranging seven miles outward almost to the city limits.

A warm, sultry wind fanned scores of fires, and in at least one area the fire ranged in a solid sheet for more than 10 blocks.

[At least four persons were reported killed, according to United Press International.]

The police arrested more than 600 adults and 100 juveniles.

But thousands more ignored a curfew of 9 P.M. to 5:30 A.M. imposed by Mr. Romney and Detroit's Mayor, Jerome P. Cavanagh. Officials ordered all schools closed today.

War Zone

"It looks like a city that has been bombed," Mr. Romney said while sweeping by helicopter over areas laid to waste by looters and arsonists.

Scores were injured, many from stabbings, but no deaths were reported early today. Sporadic gunfire was heard in the city.

A first wave of 700 National Guardsmen, 200 State Police troopers and 600 Detroit policemen failed to slow the outbreak.

Destruction spread from a West Side area where it began early yesterday and ignited flareups throughout the day and night that reached into East Side neighborhoods.

The trouble began when the police raided a "blind pig," or after hours drinking spot, on 12th Street near Clairmount and arrested 73 persons.

Mr. Romney declared a state of public emergency in Detroit and its two self-contained suburbs, Highland Park and Hamtramck.

He ordered sales halted on all liquor, beer and other alcoholic beverages as groups of Negroes grabbed liquor from stores and drank beer on some of the city's main streets.

"The disturbance is still not under control," the Governor said shortly before midnight.

The police at first were ordered to withhold gunfire, but Mr. Cavanagh said later: "Their safety is at stake, and if they must return fire, it must be."

A battalion of 800 National Guardsmen was ordered from Grand Rapids, 150 miles northwest of Detroit, to assist the 700 on duty as Mr. Romney declared the riot out of control.

Helicopters equipped with floodlights and manned by officers armed with submachineguns whirred through the fire-streaked darkness in search of rooftop snipers.

Mr. Romney said, "It's a case of lawlessness and hoodlumism and apparently not organized. Disobedience to the law cannot and will not be tolerated in Michigan."

"I will supply whatever manpower the city needs to handle the situation."

Fires raged through tenement buildings, businesses and individual residences in a mile-square section of the city's near West Side. More fires erupted in the Northwest Side.

National Guardsmen and state troopers encircled various police stations.

Inside, officers scurried up and down hallways with armloads of .38-caliber ammunition for police revolvers.

The police, however, were ordered to hold their fire. This apparently was the reason that injuries were kept to a minimum and no deaths were reported.

Fifteen of the injured were policemen, who, throughout the day-long disturbance, gave ground to the Negroes and ignored most looting.

As National Guardsmen rolled into areas of violence in Army trucks and city-owned buses, violence sprang ahead of them, surging into new areas.

The police, meanwhile, brought in carloads of guns picked up from gun stores and pawn shops in and around the riot areas and throughout the downtown section near police headquarters.

The headquarters itself was ringed with armed policemen.

City in Flames

Great clouds of smoke from flaming tenements and shattered businesses and homes lay over much of the city as dusk came,

*Police and National Guardsmen drop tear gas down an open manhole
during the riots of 1967 in an attempt to flush out a shooting suspect.*

and the smell of smoke pervaded the night air.

A four-mile section of Woodward was plundered by looters
and a three-mile section of Grand River was hit by looting and
firebombing, which raged along 18 blocks of 12th Street.

A 20-block area of Grand River was almost solidly aflame.

During the violence along 12th Street, some looters raced past
weary firemen and dropped off two six-packs of beer as a prank-
ish gesture.

At one point, beleaguered firemen pulled out of the blazing
areas, saying that they had insufficient protection from bricks,
bottles and other debris thrown at them.

They left their hoses in the streets.

Block-long sections of tenements and small businesses went
up in smoke.

Later, firemen moved back into the areas, sometimes with the
protection of residents of the burning areas.

About 20 Negro members of one block club armed themselves

with rifles and deployed around firefighters to protect them from harassment.

"They say they need protection," said Lennon Moore, one of the block club members, "and we're damn well going to give it to them."

The outbreak was the worst in Detroit since the city's race riots in 1943. Major parks, including Belle Isle, an island park, where the 1943 riot began, were closed this afternoon.

Looters roamed freely within swirls of smoke in the embattled area, carrying clothes, lamps, golf bags and other goods from flaming shops and stores with their fronts bashed in.

Detroit policemen were ordered on 24-hour duty.

II

July 27, 1967

Detroit's four-day riot appeared to be ending today. Only an occasional sniper shot broke the silence this evening in the city's riot areas. A 9 P.M. to 5:30 A.M. curfew in the city was lifted early this morning, but then reimposed because of the many sightseers who poured into the destruction zones. . . .

The city's major downtown stores were all open today, and it became a little harder, but not impossible, to find a free parking slot in downtown Detroit. . . .

The Aftermath

So far the riot, worst in the nation's recent history, has claimed 38 lives. One of the latest to die was George Messeulina, 68 years old, a white shoe repairman, who was one of the first victims of the riot. He was beaten by a Negro gang Sunday afternoon, the first day of the looting, burning, and sniping.

Riot-torn streets, such as Grand River Avenue, were jammed today with sight-seeing motorists. City bulldozers, cranes and cleaning crews knocked down walls and were moving debris in the hardest-hit areas.

Soldiers were ordered to sheathe their bayonets. However, soldiers, guardsmen and convoys of policemen continued to patrol through the city and stand guard at public buildings. There has been no indication thus far that the military forces will be removed.

Many soldiers left their bayonets out despite orders, and a ban against the sale of alcoholic beverages and gasoline in contain-

ers continued. The city authorities, however, turned their attention to rebuilding the city.

A second man, Caleb Moore, a Negro, was found dead of un-
known causes in jail.

Property damage has been estimated at more than $200-
million. More than 1,000 have been injured, 5,000 persons including juveniles have been jailed, 1,700 stores looted, and 1,383
buildings set afire.

The clean-up is moving quickly. Piles of brick and rubble have
been cleared from the streets and sidewalks in the riot areas, often pushed into the gaping holes that once were basements.

Broken glass has been swept from the sidewalks. All streets in
the city are open to traffic today, Mayor Cavanagh said, but the
signs of destruction still are visible. . . .

Economic Damage

Louis Morgan, business manager, gave this account:

"There was a sniper somewhere around. The police really shot
us up. They did all the damage. The people living upstairs got
out, thank God."

"We've got to decide what to do, fix it up or move out. This
place feeds about 50 people," Mr. Morgan said. Repairing the
damage will cost $35,000 or $40,000, and it is unlikely that the
store, if repaired, would be able to get insurance, Melvin Jefferson, the owner, said.

At Honest Joe's clothing store, which stood safe and unlooted
on 12th Street Tuesday but burned last night, broken mannequins
lay grotesquely in the windows and a small fire continued to burn
this afternoon.

At the Reliable Rug Company, a furniture store on 12th near
Clairmount, the son of the owner stood among the blackened
rubble while a workman tried to pry open the safe.

"This is it. Forget it. Who needs this," he said, predicting that
the business would not be rebuilt. The store was one of the first
to go Sunday. "They wanted the TV's," he said bitterly.

On Linwood and Pingree, three-quarters of a mile west, one
house stands near the corner. At the site where the next eight homes
stood, there is now nothing but a row of blackened chimneys.

"The fire leaped over our house from the rug cleaner's on Linwood," said Dalton Blackburn. "If I hadn't watered this place it
would have gone."

"The fire trucks came in Sunday but they ran them out with bottles," Mr. Blackburn went on, "but thank goodness, thank God for that fireman, he put some water on this house. I was working at the rug cleaner's. My job is gone."

III

Whether Detroit, two years after the worst urban upheaval in 20th century America, has recovered or learned anything from its devastating experience remains an open question. Viewed from the perspective of the black community, many of the signs are hopeful. The rhetoric of the first few months has gradually been replaced by substantial efforts, created and led by black community leaders and financed in large measure by their white counterparts, to establish black-owned businesses and housing developments. Growing political solidarity is also evident, with new coalitions formed to challenge the traditional political machinery and alliances of the city. Post-riot studies continue to affirm a significant commitment on the part of the majority of Detroit's black populace to the goal of an integrated community, but this traditional goal is balanced by a more introspective concern with the development of a strong, viable black community, with an ability to enter into bi-racial dialogue from a position of strength rather than a posture of accommodation.

The city itself, however, remains a paradox. Viewed from this broader perspective, Detroit reflects a paralysis of nerve and effort. Most of the liberal-progressive premises on which its social and economic programs had been based in the five years before the riot were called into grave question by that event, and no new premises or programs have emerged to take their place. The sweeping recommendations of the Mayor's Development Team for the reorganization of city government remain unimplemented, leadership from city hall seems increasingly ineffective, polarization between Detroit's black and white community continues to harden, and liberal elements in the city appear confused and uncertain in which direction to move. And while inertia grips political and civic leadership, the problems of crime continue to mount, business accelerate their flight from the central city to the suburbs, the schools face financial disaster, and rumors of tax increases abound. In 24 months the city of hope has become the city in crisis.

The Appointment of Justice Thurgood Marshall

By Michael D. Davis and Hunter R. Clark

On October 2, 1967, Thurgood Marshall became the first African American named to the United States Supreme Court. A successful attorney in several notable Supreme Court cases, Marshall's crowning achievement was as a prosecuting attorney in the *Brown v. Board of Education* decision, in which the "separate but equal" doctrine was found to be unconstitutional. Marshall also served as legal director of the National Association for the Advancement of Colored People (NAACP) for twenty years. During his tenure with the NAACP, Marshall focused on the directive of eliminating segregation in American schools. Nominated to the Supreme Court by President Lyndon Johnson, Marshall was famous for his quick wit and liberal point of view.

As a Supreme Court justice, Thurgood Marshall fought vehemently against the death penalty, supported a woman's right to choose an abortion, and consistently voted to uphold basic First Amendment rights. In the following excerpt from their biography of Marshall, authors Michael D. Davis and Hunter R. Clark give a brief summary of the days leading up to his historic nomination to the Supreme Court.

Thurgood Marshall would remain on the Supreme Court until his retirement in 1991. He died in 1993, leaving behind a legacy of service to the cause of civil rights and a lifetime of protecting the judicial process.

Cissy Marshall was at home on June 13, 1967, a weekday like any other. She got up and made eggs and bacon for her husband and their two sons, now eleven and eight. Then she drove her husband to the Justice Department and headed uptown with the boys to the Georgetown Day School, an exclusive private school on MacArthur Boulevard in upper northwest Washington. She returned home to the rented town house in the city's southwest quadrant and was engaged in housekeeping chores when, at around 11:00 A.M., the phone rang. It was her husband, calling from the Oval Office of the White House.

A Call from the White House

"Take a deep breath and sit down slowly," Thurgood told her. "Now, wait just a minute." The next voice on the line was that of President Johnson, telling her that he had asked her husband to join the Supreme Court.

"Mr. President, I am simply speechless," said the wife of the justice designate. She was glad she had sat down and taken a deep breath. "Thank you for having so much faith in my husband."

Later, when the joy and excitement subsided, she was able to contemplate developments from a more mundane perspective. She commented wryly, "I drive Thurgood to work and then take the boys on to school. I enjoy it. I doubt that our lives will change very much because of this appointment."

Her younger son, inspired by his father's success, told his mother, "Mom, I want to be a judge, too, when I grow up." He added, "But can't I let my hair grow long right now like the Monkees?". . .

Part of Johnson's Plans

Warned by Johnson to keep his remarks short in order to avoid controversy pending Senate hearings on his nomination, Marshall appeared laid back, almost laconic, when he stepped forward to address reporters. Asked to grade his performance as solicitor general, he replied, "I guess it's been about as good as anybody else's, maybe better than some." When he was bombarded with a barrage of other inquiries on a wide range of subjects, the nominee demurred, saying simply, "The president speaks for me."

Dozens of men have served on the U.S. Supreme Court. The historical significance of Marshall's nomination was that he was the first African American to do so. Yet there, in the Rose Garden, no reference was made to Marshall's race. Later, Senate minority leader Everett Dirksen predicted Marshall's speedy confirmation by the Senate, telling reporters, "He's a good lawyer. The fact of his color should make no difference."

Yet whether they cared to admit it or not, his color made all the difference, both to his supporters and detractors. For his part, Johnson saw Marshall's nomination as a way to revive his flagging social agenda for the Great Society, a booming, vibrant America unfettered by poverty and racial discrimination. Lady Bird was right: Her husband had done a lot for blacks.

Shortly after his landslide victory over Barry Goldwater, Johnson signed the Civil Rights Act of 1964, the most sweeping civil rights legislation of the modern era. He then pushed through Congress the Voting Rights Act of 1965. At the bill's nationally televised signing ceremony in the Capitol Rotunda, Johnson addressed the nation's black citizens directly.

"To every Negro in this country" he said, "You must vote. Your future, and your children's future, depend upon it. If you do this, then you will find, as others have found before you, that the vote is the most powerful instrument ever devised by man for breaking down injustice and destroying the terrible walls which imprison men because they are different from other men.". . .

By 1967, however, the president's social policies no longer enjoyed an enthusiastic mandate. Rioting in the nation's urban centers had fueled a white backlash that threatened racial progress. . . .

In the wake of the riots in Watts, Detroit, Newark, and other cities, Johnson was shocked to find among the moderate black leadership—including Martin Luther King Jr., the Urban League's Whitney Young, and Roy Wilkins, head of the NAACP—an utter sense of powerlessness to control or even influence young blacks in the ghettos. Johnson saw a critical need to bolster the stature of moderate black leaders and to show that, frustrating though the pace of progress might be, gradualism was in fact producing concrete results. Johnson counted on translating these results into black votes in his 1968 reelection effort. . . .

"When I appointed Thurgood Marshall to the Supreme Court," Johnson told [his biographer Doris Kearns] Goodwin, "I figured he'd be a great example to younger kids. There was probably not a Negro in America who didn't know about Thurgood's appointment. All over America that day Negro parents looked at their children a little differently, thousands of mothers looked across the breakfast table and said: 'Now maybe this will happen to my child someday.' I bet from one coast to the other there was a rash of new mothers naming their newborn sons Thurgood."

Goodwin's research showed otherwise. In her book *Lyndon Johnson and the American Dream*, she noted that birth certificates on file in New York City and Boston "revealed seven Martins, ten Luthers, eleven George Washingtons, and fifteen Franklin Delanos, but not a single Thurgood."

Blacks were, in fact, divided over the nomination, to the extent that they even knew or cared about it. Some militants were elated. Floyd McKissick, director of CORE [Congress of Racial Equality], declared, "This has stirred pride in the breast of every black American."

Thurgood Marshall

But others dismissed Marshall's appointment as a cynical act. One man's role model is another man's token. The week the nomination was announced, deadly racial disturbances rocked Tampa, Florida, and Cincinnati and Dayton, Ohio. . . .

Privately, President Johnson began to wonder whether he could get his nominee confirmed by the Senate.

The southerners on the Senate Judiciary Committee plotted their anti-Marshall strategy. They would not use Marshall's color—at least not explicitly—as the basis for their opposition to him. Instead, they would try to paint him as a liberal who was soft on crime. . . .

Confirmation Hearings

The confirmation hearings wore on for five days, July 13, 14, 18, 19, and 24, 1967. The questioning ranged from the penetrating to the absurd, from the philosophical to the kind of esoterica found in a law school exam. At one point Marshall was asked, "Do you know who drafted the Thirteenth Amendment to the U.S. Constitution?" He could not remember. At another point he was asked to explain, "Of what significance do you believe it is that in deciding the constitutional basis of the Civil Rights Act of 1866, Congress copied the enforcement provisions of this legislation from the Fugitive Slave Law of 1850?"

Marshall maintained his composure, punctuating his testimony with acerbic wit. He insisted that recent Supreme Court decisions were not responsible for any rise in the nation's crime rate. "I don't believe that any court decisions, by the decisions themselves, have increased crime," he declared.

Beyond that, he refused to discuss any matter that he might have to rule on as a member of the Court. He asked rhetorically, "Any statement I make . . . would oblige me to disqualify myself in those cases, would it not?"

The southerners were incensed. Senator Sam J. Ervin of North Carolina demanded to know, "How can this committee, or how can the Senate, perform its duty and ascertain what your constitutional or judicial philosophy is without ascertaining what you think about the Constitution?"

Marshall told him, "Well, one way, you can look at my opinions.". . .

When the hearings were finally over, the committee majority commented in its report, "There probably has never been any nominee for any judicial position who has received more minute and searching examination." By an eleven-to-five vote, the committee recommended full Senate confirmation. The majority report concluded, "The Senate will do itself honor, the Court will be graced, and the nation benefited by our confirmation of this nominee to the Supreme Court.". . .

A Justice at Last

On August 30, 1967, the Senate confirmed Marshall's appointment by the overwhelming margin of sixty-nine to eleven. Senate majority leader Mike Mansfield of Montana called the action "a confirmation of the vitality of the democratic system." He added, "Thurgood Marshall's rise to the Supreme Court reaffirms the American ideal that what counts is what you are and not who you are, or whom your antecedents may have been."

Republican senator Thomas H. Kuchel of California made a rare direct reference to Marshall's race. He called Marshall's confirmation "part of a larger process in which not only Negro Americans but Americans from all minority racial and religious backgrounds have begun to participate in the affairs of the nation."

From his office at the Justice Department, Marshall issued a statement saying he was "greatly honored by the appointment and its confirmation." He went on, "Let me take this opportunity to reaffirm my deep faith in this nation and its people and to pledge that I shall be ever mindful of my obligation to the Constitution and to the goal of equal justice under law."

Ironically, while Marshall was expressing his faith and gratitude, another black American, Stokely Carmichael, was on the other side of the world communicating contradictory sentiments. On the same day that the Senate approved Marshall's appointment to the Supreme Court, Carmichael met in Hanoi with leaders of the North Vietnamese National Assembly. He told them that U.S. blacks and the Vietnamese people were engaged in a struggle against a common enemy: U.S. imperialism. He pledged to the leaders American blacks' support.

After issuing his formal statement to the press, Marshall telephoned the president to thank him personally for the appointment. He was disappointed and somewhat perplexed to discover that Johnson did not share his unbridled enthusiasm. Johnson told him, "Well, congratulations, but the hell you caused me. Goddammit, I never went through so much hell."

Years later, in January 1973, Johnson spoke with Marshall by phone from his Texas ranch. The men had developed a friendship, combining their similar political views with their passions for bourbon and cigarettes. The former president told Marshall that he believed appointing the first black to the Supreme Court caused his political demise. "He thought that moving me here [to the Court] was what killed him off," Marshall recalls. "He felt they used the Vietnam War as the excuse. He told me that as late as about a week before he died."

"I loved that man," Marshall said of LBJ.

Meanwhile, Cissy Marshall began to peruse interior design magazines and started window-shopping for ideas. It would fall to her to decorate her husband's new chambers at the Supreme Court. What did Thurgood know about chairs, rugs, and draperies? The royal blue decor chosen by Marshall's predecessor Tom Clark would have to go. She decided instead on deep red with black leather. But for the time being, all of that would have to wait. She and the boys would have to prepare for the swearing-in ceremony.

The Haight-Ashbury Scene

By Barney Hoskyns

San Francisco has long been considered one of the most progressive
cities in the United States. With its vibrant port, thriving intellectual
centers, and eclectic artists, San Francisco quickly became the city that
exemplified the "alternative" movement in the late 1960s. Home of
several artistic and social schools of thought, San Francisco was considered the breeding ground of the popular culture that inspired the
"hippie" movement.

Setting the stage for San Francisco's rise into the top echelon of
popular culture was the "beat" movement of the fifties, which rebelled
against the ideals of conservative America. According to author and
historian Barney Hoskyns, writer of *Beneath the Diamond Sky:
Haight-Ashbury, 1965–1970,*

> The Beats made North Beach the most exciting ghetto in North
> America, howling and hollering their defiant, Whitmanesque ex-
> hortations to anyone who'd listen. They were mostly writers,
> with a sprinkling of artists and musicians at the fringes, and they
> mobilized themselves around Allen Ginsberg, Jack Kerouac, and
> William Burroughs. They got their name from an expression Ker-
> ouac picked up from a New York low-lifer who used it as a slang
> term for beaten-down, or exhausted, though Kerouac would
> claim that the word also carried connotations of beatitude.

> As the beat movement became passé, young and hip artists, college

students, intellectuals, and soul-searchers began seeking new ways to express themselves. Open-mindedness gave way to experimentation as new, mind-altering drugs and hallucinogens were gaining notoriety. The foremost of these "new" substances was LSD, or acid, a drug notably endorsed by Harvard professor Timothy Leary as well as San Francisco fixture Ken Kesey, author of the famed novel *One Flew Over the Cuckoo's Nest.*

The proverbial home base of this experimentation and the ensuing shift in popular culture was the famous neighborhood of Haight-Ashbury, a blue-collar, racially diverse area near San Francisco State University. Some of the most notable musical artists of the era, including the Grateful Dead, Janis Joplin, and Jefferson Airplane were firmly rooted in the Haight-Ashbury scene. Additionally, noted social groups such as the Diggers implemented communal living situations in an attempt to combat the ideals of a society they saw as insensitive and capitalistic. The Digger movement was successful for some time, notes Hoskyns in *Beneath the Diamond Sky:*

> The Diggers most radical initiative was to distribute free food in the Panhandle every afternoon, a response to the swelling ranks of homeless and impoverished teenagers flooding the Haight. They would scour market stalls and supermarket bins every day for discarded food, turning their spoils into soup. Many store-owners accepted the Diggers as the unofficial conscience of the streets.

In its glory days, the Haight was considered at the forefront of progressive thinking. However, by 1967, as the notoriety of the neighborhood grew, an influx of people began to degrade overall quality of life. Drug use in the Haight was rampant, and social ideals became corrupted by domestic strife and poverty. In October 1967, the Diggers sponsored the "Death of the Hippie" march, symbolizing the corruption of the social experiment that was Haight-Ashbury at its peak. The music of the era lives on, echoing a time of progressive thinking and experimentation.

In the following additional passages from his 1997 book *Beneath the Diamond Sky*, Barney Hoskyns explores the incredible social melting pot that was Haight-Ashbury in 1967.

Nineteen sixty-seven was a year of great landmarks in the worlds of rock and hippiedom. In San Francisco, it began with a magical congregation in the Polo Grounds of Golden Gate Park. The "Human Be-In," the so-called "gathering of the tribes," had been conceived by the editors of the *San Francisco Oracle* as a way of uniting the myriad entities which comprised the hippie underground. "Berkeley political activists and the love generation of Haight-Ashbury," announced the press release, "will join together with members of the new nation who will be coming from every state in the nation, every tribe of the young . . . TO POW-WOW, CELEBRATE, AND PROPHESY THE EPOCH OF LIBERATION, LOVE, PEACE, COMPASSION, AND UNITY OF MANKIND." Grateful Dead manager Rock Scully noted that "we have invited the Berkeley rads because we consider them outlaws like ourselves, but we make it a condition of their participating that there be ABSOLUTELY NO RABBLE-ROUSING."

Gathering of the Tribes

Advertised by a Rick Griffin poster that featured psychedelic Western lettering and a guitar-toting Native American warrior on a horse, the "pow-wow" promised a lineup of Frisco bands and campus firebrands, of Beat legends and psychedelic gurus. Indeed, one could almost argue that the event had been commandeered by a group of aging bohemians (Ginsberg, Leary, Ferlinghetti, Snyder, Rubin, et al.) who wanted to ensure they obtained an "in" with the new generation—especially since Leary, for one, was regarded by denizens of the Haight with suspicion. But it would be churlish to argue thus, considering how genuinely united the twenty thousand-odd people traipsing through Golden Gate Park on that golden winter morning of January 14 felt.

For Ginsberg, the Be-In was like [poet William] Blake's vision of Eden: A shimmering sea of smiling faces, many belonging to people flying high on Owsley's new "White Lightning" acid. MC'd by Buddha, a Haight scenester and crony of Big Brother, the gathering was a peak moment of Utopian hippie bliss. "A lot of stoned people were wandering around blowing their minds on how many others were there," wrote Charles Perry. "It was like awakening to find you'd been reborn and this was your new family." Perry called it "one of the grand mythic events of the Haight mystique . . . the notion of a meeting without any purpose other than to be," and Steve Levine of the *Oracle* wrote that it was "a calm and peaceful approbation, a reaffirmation of the life spirit, a settling of the waters." In the midst of it all sat Timothy Leary, grinning helplessly in white cotton with petals tucked behind his ear.

Musical Legends of the Haight

Among the Berkeley contingent at the Be-In, significantly, were Country Joe and the Fish, the band whose music itself bridged the gulf between the hippies and the radicals. Back in June '66 the Fish had recorded an eponymous three-track EP that ranks among the first true psychedelic recordings to come out of the Bay Area. "Thing Called Love" was generic garage blues-rock, but "Bass Strings" and "Section 43" were trippy, eerily mesmerizing. "Got so high this time that you know/I'll never come down," Joe McDonald sang in his softest, spaciest voice on "Bass Strings." The instrumental "Section 43" was inspired by "The Hall of the Mountain King" in Peer Gynt, but the mesh of Barry Melton's rippling guitar runs and David Cohen's haunting organ pads created a druggy, almost Eastern quality. "No one had ever heard something like 'Section 43' or 'Bass Strings' before," McDonald said later. "At the moment of that EP we were the only people in the world doing that, an aspect of us that hasn't really be acknowledged." After the EP, even the formerly scathing *Berkeley Barb* began to rally to the Haight cause of rock and drugs and free love.

When the Fish set to work on their first Vanguard album their approach was similarly low on politics, high on acid poetics. Released in April '67, *Electric Music for the Mind and Body* was a psychedelic masterwork, a freaky lysergic journey featuring reworked versions of all three EP tracks, along with the exquisite "Porpoise Mouth," the chilling "Death Sound," and a hymn to the lead singer of the Jefferson Airplane called "Grace." "I think *Electric Music* is the best psychedelic record ever made," says McDonald modestly. "Millions of people have tripped to that album. It's guaranteed!"

McDonald completed his "crossing" from Berkeley to the Haight when he commenced an affair with the new princess of the San Francisco underground—or "the first hippie pinup girl," as Janis Joplin had now been dubbed. Not long after Big Brother and the Holding Company manager Julius Karpen moved the band back to the city from Lagunitas early in 1967, Janis began living with McDonald in a small apartment on Lyon Street. The relationship was fated to peter out—he liked acid, she preferred Southern Comfort—but for the time it was a notable celebrity coupling.

With Big Brother now established as a regular fixture at the Avalon, Joplin was transforming herself into rock royalty. Swathed in silk and velvet, bedecked in bangles and feather boas, she wasn't interested in San Francisco anonymity. She wanted to be a star in the way that Mick Jagger was a star. She had also found her very own showstopper in the form of Willie Mae "Big Mama" Thornton's harrowing "Ball and Chain." Catching Thornton singing one night in a little joint on Divisadero Street, she went backstage to ask if she could use the song, which was perfect material for the persona of the tragic, hard-bitten blues mama Joplin was so keen to cultivate. Big Mama said she was welcome to it.

Other leading San Francisco bands were busy in the studio. Both the Grateful Dead and the Jefferson Airplane were cutting albums at RCA-Victor in Los Angeles: The Dead their first and the Airplane their second, both with producer Dave Hassinger. Recorded in three days on a speed marathon, *The Grateful Dead* was an unsatisfying compromise between the group's glorified-bar-band origins and their desire for free-flowing experimentation, produced by a man who was irredeemably square, in an unsympathetic Hollywood environment of velour and Naugahyde. Still, you could hear the Dead's sheer exuberance in the opening "The Golden Road (To Unlimited Devotion)," the first single, and in the versions of "Viola Lee Blues" and "Sitting On Top Of The World." "In the land of the dark," trumpeted the ad in the *Oracle*, "the ship of the sun is piloted by the Grateful Dead."

The Airplane's *Surrealistic Pillow* was a much more confident album, boasting two Top 10 singles in the revamped Great Society songs "Somebody to Love" and "White Rabbit." Ironically, [Grateful Dead member] Jerry Garcia was credited on the record as "musical and spiritual advisor": He had sat in on the sessions at the Victor studios and his input on the album's arrangements (and its title, come to that) was deemed by all concerned to have made the crucial difference to its success. . . . Released with much accompanying fanfare in March 1967, it climbed as high as No. 3 on the album chart and confirmed the Airplane's status as the preeminent San Francisco band. For [Jefferson Airplane singer Grace] Slick, in particular, it was a triumph: [Marty] Balin was a good singer, but Slick's strident tone was the band's new hallmark. . . .

Along with the new bands came a revolutionary new radio format on the FM waveband. In February, 1967, deejay Larry Miller started playing underground rock tracks on his all-night show on KMPX; in April, Tom Donahue took over an earlier slot on the station. By the summer, KMPX was broadcasting hippie music twenty-four hours a day—much to the distaste of conservative programmers like Bill Drake, who wouldn't add Country Joe and the Fish's "Not So Sweet Lorraine" to his KHJ playlist in L.A. despite the fact that it had hit No. 1 on his San Francisco station. Drake claimed that the San Francisco "scene" was a myth, "magnifying itself basically on fumes.". . .

Summer of Love

As the "Summer of Love" became a reality, the outside world moved in for the kill. *Time* put together a special issue, and *Life* ran a major feature entitled "The New Rock: Music That's Hooked the Whole Vibrating World." Hollywood churned out exploitation movies like Roger Corman's *The Trip* and Sam Katzman's *The Love-Ins.* By April, the Gray Line bus company was including a "Hippie Hop" tour of the Haight among its San Francisco attractions. Kids were swarming into San Francisco *en masse*, many of them panhandling for money, some taking part-time jobs like mail-sorting. Along Haight Street there was a permanent "revue" of hippie performers. "There will always be at least one man with long hair and sunglasses playing a wooden pipe," wrote [journalist] Hunter S. Thompson in the *New York Times Magazine* in May. "[And] a hairy blond fellow wearing a Black Bart cowboy hat playing bongos . . . and a dazed-looking girl wearing a blouse but no bra." Drugs, Thompson concluded, had made formal entertainment obsolete in the "Hashbury."

Also swarming into the Haight, unfortunately, were all manner of creepy and nefarious characters: Dealers, cultists, general leeches. The Haight-Ashbury Research Project, launched the following year, calculated that 15 percent of the people who'd drifted into the area in 1967 were "psychotic fringe and religious obsessives." When budding Hollywood groupie Pamela Des

Barres checked out the Haight in January, she hung out with a street freak called "Bummer Bob," who played bouzouki in an outfit known as the Chamber Orkustra. Later he would be better known as Charles Manson acolyte Bobby Beausoleil. (Manson himself spent time in the Haight, allegedly living on the roof of the Straight Theater and recruiting a few damaged hippie chicks to his retinue while he was there. Sandy Good had been one of the original Deadheads at the Acid Tests and the Trips Festival.)

Sense of Menace

Two months later, writer Joan Didion visited from Los Angeles and was alarmed by the pervasive sense of menace in the community. As she noted in her famous piece "Slouching Towards Bethlehem," drug users were already forsaking acid for the joys of shooting crystal methedrine; those who *were* still tripping were having a lot of bummers. Where there was crystal meth, moreover, heroin soon followed to cushion the comedown: Even [Digger] Emmett Grogan started messing with smack in the summer (he would die of an overdose on the New York City subway on April Fool's Day, 1978). For Didion, quoting from Yeats' famous poem "The Second Coming," "the center was not holding."

Among the various tensions beginning to surface in the Haight as spring turned into summer and the population swelled was a new friction between white hippies and black residents of the Fillmore district that lay to the south. Black teenagers accosted white longhairs who wandered through their neighborhood and sometimes physically attacked them. Beat veteran Chester Anderson, who published a regular bulletin with the title *Com/co*, called the Haight "the first segregated bohemia I've ever seen." More generally, Anderson could report that "rape is as common as bullshit on Haight Street," and that "minds and bodies are being maimed as we watch a scale model of Vietnam." Hepatitis and gonorrhea were spreading; health inspectors, worried about epidemics, issued a violation warning to a Digger crash pad. The Diggers themselves had taken to carrying guns around, and *Com/co* announced that "An Armed Man Is a Free Man." Love was the password in the Hashbury, noted Hunter Thompson, "but paranoia is the style." Elder statesmen like Gary Snyder were already recommending that hippies "tribalize" and live communally outside the city.

Dwindling Optimism

Five months after the "hippietopian" promise of the Human Be-In, Country Joe and the Fish manager Ed Denson admitted that he was "very pessimistic" about the hippie movement. "Right now it's good for a lot of people," he said, "but I have to look back at the Berkeley scene. There was a tremendous optimism there too, but look where all that went. The Beat Generation? Where are they now? What about hula-hoops? Maybe this hippie thing is more than a fad . . . but I'm not optimistic. If the hippies were more realistic they'd stand a better chance of surviving."

For his part, police chief Cahill—the man who'd actually coined the corny phrase "the love generation"—was more blunt. "Hippies are no asset to the community," he said. "These people do not have the courage to face the realities of life.". . .

On October 6, 1967, a year after the "Love Pageant Rally" in the Hashbury, the Diggers organized a "Death of Hippie" march along Haight Street, a parade that concluded with the burial of the sign which had hung outside the Psychedelic Shop. "The media cast nets, create bags for the identity-hungry to climb in," the Digger press release ranted. "Your face on TV, your style immortalized without soul . . . the free man vomits his images and laughs in the clouds. . . ."

A general exodus from Haight-Ashbury was beginning, as people left to "get it together in the country" in the hippie communes. What [promoter] Bill Graham called the "general hope" of the Haight's heyday had died. In the words of Derek Taylor—who'd enjoyed a blissful trip at Monterey on Owsley's "Purple Haze"—"people always fuck up in the end."

Stop the Draft Week

By Tom Wells

Nineteen sixty-seven was a year that saw a vast increase in the numbers, effectiveness, and seriousness of civil disobedience and protest. Several different grassroots social protest groups came to national prominence during this time, due partly to the high-profile, media-savvy nature of their demonstrations.

Stop the Draft Week (STDW), which began on October 16, 1967, in Oakland, California, was one of the events which attracted considerable attention. At the roots of STDW were members of various antiwar groups—such as the Student Nonviolent Coordinating Committee (SNCC) and the Students for a Democratic Society (SDS)—who became known as the aptly named "the Resistance." Joined by the growing number of individuals who believed the draft was unconstitutional and class biased, the Resistance sponsored draft-card burnings and turn-ins, prompting a reexamination of the social effects and implications of the draft. Stop the Draft Week was the culmination of the Resistance's efforts to raise awareness about the government's pursuit of war in Vietnam.

In an excerpt from his 1994 book *The War Within: America's Battle over Vietnam*, historian Tom Wells gives an overview of the forces behind STDW.

O ver the winter and spring of 1967, dark clouds of outright resistance to the war were gathering. By March there were some two dozen "We Won't Go" groups on college campuses, members of which pledged to refuse service in Vietnam. Counseling centers on conscientious objection run by the AFSC [American Friends Service Committee] and other pacifist groups were attracting thousands of youths. Many black youths were rejecting induction orders. The draft was simply "white people sending black people to make war on yellow people in order to defend the land they stole from red people," SNCC's Stokely Carmichael observed. A number of white youths had also refused induction or publicly destroyed their draft cards.

The National Council of SDS adopted a resolution encouraging draft resistance. "We sat down and purposely read all the laws around the draft so that we could violate every single one of them," SDS Vice President Carl Davidson, the main author of the resolution, humorously remembered. "We wanted to . . . come up with a program that was *totally* illegal." To many SDS-ers at the meeting, it was unnecessary to put the resolution up for a formal vote. "After going back and forth on the legality of this question," Davidson said, "finally after seventeen hours we decided, if this was so illegal, why did we need a resolution passed in order to support it? We should just go out and do it. We sort of took our anarchism to its logical conclusion."

The Resistance Is Born

Activists at Cornell University began planning a national draft-card burning. Veterans of a lively anti-rank sit-in in the spring of 1966, they had formed one of the country's first We Won't Go groups early that fall. The group emphasized slow, grass-roots organizing over public protest. . . .

Three thousand miles away, a national organization of draft resisters was independently taking shape. Early on the morning of March 8, David Harris, who had earlier returned to the government several draft cards bearing his name, met with his friend Dennis Sweeney and the Berkeley antiwar activists Steve Hamilton and Lennie Heller. Sitting in the rickety communal house Harris and Sweeney shared with a handful of others in East Palo Alto, California, smoking "a lot of dope," the four youths talked of holding a national draft-card turn-in in the fall. Hamilton and Heller had come prepared for serious organizing. They handed Harris and Sweeney some literature with the name "The Resistance" printed on it. This prospective name for their new group pointed to the resistance in Europe to Nazi occupation during

World War II. Hamilton and Heller felt the war would soon bring fascistic political conditions to the United States. They were not alone. As Bettina Aptheker remembered, in 1967 "when you said the word *resistance*, it was with a capital *R*, and you meant the resistance to fascism in Europe. . . . People had a sense of very great repression in this country. . . . People felt like fascism was creeping in on us from a lot of different directions." Inspirited by hearty conversation, the four young activists decided to move. The following month they announced the Resistance's formation and their plan to hold a national draft-card turn-in on October 16.

The upsurge in antidraft activity in early 1967 had strikingly diverse causes. Many young people had come to conclude that the whole draft system, particularly its provision for student deferments, had an unacceptable class bias. Also, signs were emerging with shocking lucidity that student deferments were oppressive themselves. *Ramparts* and *New Left Notes* publicized a memo written by SSS [Selective Service System] Director Lewis Hershey on the *real* reason for the draft system. According to Hershey, procuring manpower for the military was "not much of an administrative or financial challenge. It is in dealing with the other millions of registrants that the System is heavily occupied, developing more effective human beings in the national interest." Threatened by the "club of induction," students were being "channeled," they learned, into training and jobs deemed "essential" to the country's welfare by the same government that was waging the war. Hershey bragged:

> Many young men would not have pursued a higher education if there had not been a program of student deferment. Many young scientists, engineers, tool and die makers, and other possessors of scarce skills would not remain in their jobs in the defense effort if it were not for a program of occupational deferments.
>
> . . . From the individual's viewpoint, he is standing in a room which has been made uncomfortably warm. Several doors are open, but they all lead to various forms of recognized, patriotic service to the Nation.

The growth in public opposition to the war had also enhanced draft resistance's appeal. Many youth perceived that it would now elicit a substantial popular response. And with draft calls skyrocketing and class ranking continuing, more than a few students feared losing their deferments and receiving a one-way ticket to Vietnam. By resisting the draft they might save their skins. Conscription "was perceived as a life or death question," Carl Davidson recalled. Students felt "if they don't pass, get a good grade on this test, maybe they'll flunk out—and then they'll die."

But the single most important reason for heightened fascination with antidraft activity in 1967 was the perception that previous peace protests had exerted insufficient influence on the war. If the government would not heed legal protest, many young people reasoned, it was time to take their opposition to a deeper level. . . .

Bringing Credibility to the Movement

Resisters also maintained that noncooperation would increase protesters' credibility with the public. By challenging the government to send them to jail, resisters asserted, they were demonstrating that their opposition to the war sprang not from cowardice or youthful frivolity—as supporters of the war often alleged—but from unyielding moral convictions. Since most students came from middle-class backgrounds, the Resistance's message was directed predominately at this community. Harris explained:

> The question in the antiwar movement was how to talk to new people, how to break yourself into new audiences, and quite specifically for college students, how to bring the question of the war home to the segment of the population that they represented, which was also the principal power base of the government: the white middle class. That's where wars are made and wars are stopped. And we all came from it. I felt that in order to speak clearly to that group of people (which included my own parents, for example), it was necessary to put your body where your mouth was. You know, there was a lot of cheap talk going on in the antiwar movement: "We're against the war, we're against the war"—and then taking special privileges. And one of the first things that opponents of the antiwar movement pointed to was, "Hey, look, our young men are over in Vietnam dying, and these guys are sitting around smoking dope." I felt that in order for the antiwar movement to be effective speaking to that larger audience, it had to pay its own prices and make its own sacrifices and put itself in a position of vulnerability. Because I thought they were right, the critics were. I thought there were a lot of SDS members in Berkeley who were sitting around being tourists in the movement, myself. I don't care how radical they talked—

they weren't paying any prices. When it came down to whether they would even [refuse to] carry a draft card in their pocket, they were chickenshit. The biggest problem we had when we set out organizing was with SDS, not with the government. Because there were a lot of armchair radicals who wanted to go scream "Off the pig!" at the rally and then go hide behind their student deferments. Oh, I don't blame the rest of the public for looking down on that kind of activity. *I* look down on that kind of activity. . . . Propagandizing by example, as it were, was the only way to be taken seriously as far as I was concerned.

Through making themselves just as susceptible to the draft as poor and working-class youths, noncooperators hoped to increase their credibility among these groups as well. . . .

Resisters further believed that many Americans—including government officials—would lose enthusiasm for the war because of the "turmoil" draft resistance was wreaking in the United States. Even if the criminal justice system could process the host of lawbreakers, they maintained, their wholesale defiance of the law would suggest a society splitting at the seams. "We were going to make the country so torn about this," [Resistance activist Michael] Ferber remembered. "The universities were going to be a mess, the churches were going to be mobilized. We just felt we'd make enough trouble." The government "couldn't tolerate this kind of resistance . . . very long," he thought.

Resistance organizers hoped their courage would inspire greater commitment from the rest of the antiwar movement as well. "We were aware also that we would be a kind of spearhead," Ferber said, sparking "a lot of other groups to do less kamikaze sorts of things." If widespread prison sentences resulted, all the better. "Many of our fellows on the campus and in the community at large will then be moved to action by a fresh instance of that repression which is becoming an increasingly important factor of American life," one Resistance flyer predicted.

Finally, some resisters anticipated restricting the supply of American soldiers available for deployment to Vietnam. "Our ultimate strategy was to deny the government the troops with which to wage the war," Harris recalled. . . .

Timing the Event

As peace activists debated the political merits of noncooperation, [a] controversy was flaring over how to best channel public sup-

A group of hippies gathers to protest the draft during Stop the Draft Week in October 1967.

port for it. It reflected growing doubts among young radicals that nonviolent protests could end the war.

The four Resistance co-founders had initially agreed to ask their supporters to participate in a demonstration outside the Oakland induction center. They differed on how to build the action. Steve Hamilton thought all interested parties should collectively organize it. David Harris felt this was "the whole wrong approach." He worried that many of the Bay Area's youthful "revolutionaries" would want to battle the cops. "I knew what would happen if we brought people together and then said, 'Let's find a plan,'" Harris remembered. "Especially in . . . *Berkeley*, where there were four thousand political groups and more bullshit than you could shake a stick at." He and Dennis Sweeney believed Resistance organizers should design the demonstration.

But Hamilton doubted Harris and Sweeney would support an action militant enough to appeal to working-class youth. And he was feeling pressure from other Bay Area radicals to begin building a series of antidraft actions at the Oakland induction center October 16–20. The National Mobilization Committee . . . [another draft resistance organization] was planning a large national antiwar protest on October 21, and the close proximity between that date and the date of the turn-in seemed to offer the perfect opportunity for a solid week of resistance activities.

When Harris and Sweeney were out of town, Hamilton called a meeting to plan "Stop the Draft Week" (STDW) in Oakland. When Harris and Sweeney returned, they were "furious."

Planning STDW

The summer planning meetings for STDW were stormy, further dividing a Bay Area left already fragmented into a multitude of slivers. Many traditional pacifists wanted to sit in the doorways to the induction center. Harris advocated *decentralized* nonviolent civil disobedience. Groups of protesters should head to outlying towns where inductees were picked up and wheeled into Oakland, he exhorted. When government buses pulled up to these stops, the protesters should "whap—chain them down." After the buses were on the road toward Oakland again, other obstacles should greet them. "We were going to buy old used cars, under phony names, and get ahead of the bus on the freeway when it was going to make the turnoff," Harris reminisced. "And we were going to stop in the middle of the off-ramp. You know, park the son of a bitch, take the keys and run. And literally go for the practical effect of making it impossible for them to run the induction center that day—period."

Many radicals desired something with more bite to it. They were frustrated by the inability of nonviolent action to end the war; some had even "started playing with guns as a way to forget their own hopelessness," one recalled. These radicals also shared Hamilton's conviction that a "new kind" of militant demonstration was necessary to reach working-class youth, particularly blacks. By "defending themselves" against police attacks, they maintained, protesters would demonstrate the "strength" and "seriousness" of the middle-class antidraft movement, thereby encouraging "young workers" to resist. "Vicariously intoxicated by the summer riots" that erupted in cities across the United States, these radicals modeled their plan for STDW "after a black street rebellion." They talked of "mobility," "spontaneity," "outflanking the police," and "kicking ass." Exactly how this white riot would shut down the induction center—or end the war—was "left unanswered." Hamilton conceded, "It was all vague." . . .

Stop the Draft Week

On Monday, October 16, at 5 A.M., more than two hundred pacifists blocked the doors to the Oakland induction center. Opposed to the violent inclinations of Oakland STDW's militant organizers, the pacifists had pulled out of that committee and organized their own protest. They were methodically arrested.

Eight hours later, David Harris addressed the two thousand people congregated in front of San Francisco's federal building. A basket was being passed back through the crowd, Harris announced. The time had come: draft-age males could either be accomplices to murder or "outlaws." After three trips through the crowd, the basket returned to the front stuffed to the brim.

As the receptacle was circulating for the last time, Cecil Poole emerged from his office in the building to observe the ceremony. Dickie Harris, a black draft resister, approached the black federal attorney and asked, "Brother Poole, you head nigger here?" Harris then dumped the container of draft cards on Poole's head. Poole turned the approximately four hundred documents over to the FBI.

The same afternoon, Rev. George Williams, a Harvard divinity professor, issued a call for draft cards in the still, anxious air of Boston's Arlington Street Church.

> No one knew what would happen. Maybe fifty, or seventy-five? A trickle of men started down the aisle. . . . The aisle soon filled, the line grew longer, the doors were opened to let in those from outside who wanted to join. The organ played, flash bulbs popped, and TV cameras hummed away. It must have been twenty minutes before it was over. More than sixty burned their cards at the candle, and over two hundred handed them in.

Observing the ceremony was NBC News commentator Sander Vanocur. Tears welled up in his eyes. "What a country this would be," Vanocur told Rev. William Sloane Coffin, who had spoken at the ceremony, "if something like this were now to take place in every church." On television that night, following an excerpt from Coffin's speech, NBC's John Chancellor quietly told the nation, "If men like this are beginning to say things like this, I guess we had all better start paying attention." From twelve to fifteen hundred youths returned draft cards in eighteen cities that day. . . .

Police Reaction

Early the next morning, three thousand demonstrators converged on the Oakland induction center. It was time for the STDW militants to do their number. Some of the protesters were equipped with primitive shields and motorcycle helmets to ward off police blows. Soon a dense phalanx of cops, heads rattling with "off the pig" threats relayed to them by their undercover brethren in the STDW committee, hands clasping clubs, business faces on, their wives watching breathlessly from a nearby parking garage, advanced ominously toward the demonstrators. They "went to work on them." More than twenty people were injured (including innocent bystanders and journalists); twenty-five were arrested. By 9 A.M. the streets bordering the building had been cleared.

Forty minutes later, Joseph Califano penned a progress report on the situation to President Johnson. Although the mess in front of the induction center had been mopped up (with the aid of Mace, "which makes an individual lethargic"), Califano reported, circumstances remained "tense." Two to four thousand people were still "milling around" the area. Johnson was undoubtedly pleased when later informed that the rabble had retreated. The previous week, at his request, the president had obtained a report from the Attorney General's Office on preparations for STDW.

That night protesters held a mass meeting on the University of California campus in Berkeley to decide how to respond to the day's bloodletting. Shaken and wounded STDW leaders were "unable to run a coherent rally." Charges of police brutality and empty promises of smashing the state punctuated the session. Some speakers advocated moving on the university chancellor's office. David Harris considered this "crazy." "The Berkeley chancellor's office?" he thought to himself. "For Christ sake, these guys, they were going to 'off the pig,' I thought." The militants had turned "chickenshit," Harris perceived. "They'd gotten scared." He urged the crowd to return to the induction center for a nonviolent protest in the morning. That motion carried, and on Wednesday some four hundred people picketed the center. Ninety-one sat in its doorways and suffered arrest. There was no violence.

Violence in Madison

The scene was less placid two thousand miles away. On the University of Wisconsin campus in Madison, a throng of students strode into the Commerce Building and proclaimed an end to the job interviews being conducted there by recruiters from the Dow Chemical Company. They would leave when Dow's bagmen left. A university official initially agreed to shoo the recruiters away, but, when asked to put his commitment on paper, "lost his cool." In came the local police riot squad. Students were swiftly streaming out of the building, battered and dazed, only to be beaten again by a gauntlet of cops. The two thousand onlookers who had gathered outside, "smelling trouble as sure as any turkey buzzard," were furious at the wanton police violence. "Sieg heil," they chanted, arms upward. Many were gassed. They pelted police with rocks and bricks. When Mace failed to make the protesters lethargic, the county sheriff's office dispatched a riot team with snarling dogs. The tired and bloodied crowd gradually disbanded.

The Protests Continue

The next day several hundred protesters peacefully picketed the Oakland induction center. In neighboring Berkeley, STDW's militants made plans to hold another "new kind" of demonstration the following morning. Wednesday's action had not sat well with them. Watching frightened young draftees file into the induction center while ineffectually shouting "Don't Go" at them had been demoralizing. Their "impotence" had been "exposed." They would try to shut down the building again. But this time they would exhibit greater mobility and aggressiveness in the face of police assaults. No one would get trapped and beaten by the pigs again. The cops might even take a pounding. Steve Hamilton fixed to set up a "command central" for the assault in a hotel adjacent to the induction center. From there, STDW generals, in touch with walkie-talkie-wielding lieutenants in the field, would direct the troops to the most exploitable ground. Hamilton asked the hotel's manager for a room overlooking the center. The manager "rented us the room and immediately called the police," Hamilton recalled.

By 6 A.M. on Friday, nearly ten thousand demonstrators were gathered in the streets around the building. Many wore headgear and carried placards conveniently attached to hard wooden poles. Some had Vaseline on their faces to reduce Mace's sting. At 7 A.M. the cops launched their opening thrusts. The protesters retreated as planned, expanding the perimeter of the battle. They barricaded intersections using potted trees, garbage cans, unlocked cars. Some surrounded policemen, coercing them into harried retreats. A county bus lost its ignition wires. As they gained confidence in their ability to feint, jab, and withdraw at will, many young demonstrators began to feel like urban guerrillas. One seized a cop's baton and whacked him crisply over the head with it. "I was a little amazed at how far it went," Hamilton recalled of the protest. Hamilton was particularly stunned when an aged CPer asked him to help flip a car over. When the dust had settled, arrests and injuries were surprisingly few.

Martin Luther King Jr. Denounces the Vietnam Conflict

By Martin Luther King Jr.

Perhaps the most beloved and respected civic leader in American history, Reverend Martin Luther King Jr. is considered one of the driving forces behind the civil rights movement of the 1950s and 1960s. King's view was that African Americans could achieve civil rights and equality through nonviolent protests, and this helped the movement gain respect and acceptance.

King was not only concerned with achieving black equality. In keeping with his nonviolent philosophy, King publicly denounced the Vietnam conflict in April 1967. King's comments caused uproar, as many people considered his stance on the war to be unpatriotic.

Despite being condemned by black and white leaders and being deserted by some friends and followers, King continued to preach peaceful solutions to world conflict and speak against the war in Vietnam. The following sermon, entitled "Conscience and the Vietnam War," is demonstrative of King's speeches, which are considered the most influential and heartfelt of the turbulent decade. In the speech, aired by the Canadian Broadcasting Company during November 1967, King called for the focus of the nation to switch from overseas conflict to the plight of the poor in America.

Martin Luther King Jr., *A Testament of Hope: The Essential Writings of Martin Luther King Jr.*, edited by James Melvin Washington. San Francisco: Harper & Row, 1991. Copyright © 1968 by Dr. Martin Luther King Jr. Reproduced by arrangement with The Heirs to the Estate of Martin Luther King Jr., c/o Writers House, Inc., as agent for the proprietor, New York, NY.

It is many months now since I found myself obliged by conscience to end my silence and to take a public stand against my country's war in Vietnam. The considerations which led me to that painful decision have not disappeared; indeed, they have been magnified by the course of events since then. The war itself is intensified; the impact on my country is even more destructive.

I cannot speak about the great themes of violence and nonviolence, of social change and of hope for the future, without reflecting on the tremendous violence of Vietnam.

Since the spring of 1967, when I first made public my opposition to my government's policy, many persons have questioned me about the wisdom of my decision. "Why *you?*" they have said. "Peace and civil rights don't mix. Aren't you hurting the cause of your people?" And when I hear such questions, I have been greatly saddened, for they mean that the inquirers have never really known me, my commitment, or my calling. Indeed, that question suggests that they do not know the world in which they live.

In explaining my position, I have tried to make it clear that I remain perplexed—as I think everyone must be perplexed—by the complexities and ambiguities of Vietnam. I would not wish to underrate the need for a collective solution to this tragic war. I would wish neither to present North Vietnam or the National Liberation Front as paragons of virtue nor to overlook the role they can play in the successful resolutions of the problem. While they both may have justifiable reasons to be suspicious of the good faith of the United States, life and history give eloquent testimony to the fact that conflicts are never resolved without trustful give-and-take on both sides.

Crippled by Society

Since I am a preacher by calling, I suppose it is not surprising that I had several reasons for bringing Vietnam into the field of my moral vision. There is at the outset a very obvious and almost facile connection between the war in Vietnam and the struggle I and others have been waging in America. A few years ago there was a shining moment in that struggle. It seemed as if there was a real promise of hope for the poor, both black and white, through the poverty program. There were experiments, hopes, new beginnings. Then came the buildup in Vietnam, and I watched the program broken and eviscerated as if it were some idle political plaything of a society gone mad on war, and I knew that America would never invest the necessary funds or energies in rehabilitation of its poor so long as adventures like Vietnam continued to draw men and skills and money like some demoniacal destructive suction tube. And so I was increasingly compelled to see the war not only as a moral outrage but also as an enemy of the poor, and to attack it as such.

Perhaps a more tragic recognition of reality took place when it became clear to me that the war was doing far more than devastating the hopes of the poor at home. It was sending their sons and their brothers and their husbands to fight and die and in extraordinarily higher proportions relative to the rest of the population. We were taking the black young men who had been crippled by our society and sending them eight thousand miles away to guarantee liberties in Southeast Asia which they had not found in southwest Georgia and east Harlem. And so we have been repeatedly faced with the cruel irony of watching Negro and white boys on TV screens as they kill and die together for a nation that has been unable to seat them together in the same schools. We watch them in brutal solidarity burning the huts of a poor village, but we realize that they would never live on the same block in Detroit. I could not be silent in the face of such cruel manipulation of the poor.

My third reason moves to an even deeper level of awareness, but it grows out of my experience in the ghettos of the North over the last three years—especially the last three summers. As I have walked among the desperate, rejected, angry young men, I have told them that Molotov cocktails and rifles would not solve their problems. I have tried to offer them my deepest compassion, while maintaining my conviction that social change comes most meaningfully through nonviolent action. But, they asked, and rightly so, what about Vietnam? They asked if our own nation wasn't using massive doses of violence to solve its problems, to bring about the changes it wanted. Their questions hit home, and I knew that I could never again raise my voice against the violence of the oppressed in the ghettos without first having spoken clearly to the greatest purveyor of violence in the world today: my own government. For the sake of those boys, for the sake of this government, for the sake of the hundreds of thousands trembling under our violence, I cannot be silent. . . .

View from the Other Side

And as I ponder the madness of Vietnam and search within my-self for ways to understand and respond in compassion, my mind goes constantly to the people of that peninsula. I speak now not of the soldiers of each side, not of the junta in Saigon, but simply of the people who have been living under the curse of war for al-most three continuous decades now I think of them, too, because it is clear to me that there will be no meaningful solution until some attempt is made to know them and to hear their broken cries.

They must see the Americans as strange liberators. The Viet-namese people proclaimed their own independence in 1945 af-ter a combined French and Japanese occupation and before the Communist revolution in China. They were led by Ho Chi Minh.

Martin Luther King Jr. publicly denounced the Vietnam conflict in April 1967, an act many Americans considered unpatriotic.

Even though they quoted the American Declaration of Independence in their own document of freedom, we refused to recognize them. Our government felt then that the Vietnamese people weren't ready for independence, and we again fell victim to the deadly Western arrogance that has poisoned the international atmosphere for so long.

For nine years following 1945 we vigorously supported the French in their abortive attempt to recolonize Vietnam. After the French were defeated, it looked as if independence and land reform would come through the Geneva Agreements. But instead there came the United States, determined that Ho should not unify the temporarily divided nation, and the peasants watched again as we supported one of the most vicious modern dictators, [South Vietnam's] Premier [Ngo Dinh] Diem. The peasants watched and cringed as Diem ruthlessly rooted out all opposition, supported their extortionist landlords, and refused even to discuss reunification with the North. The peasants watched as all this was presided over by U.S. influence and then by increasing numbers of U.S. troops, who came to help quell the insurgency that Diem's methods had aroused. When Diem was overthrown, they may have been happy, but the long line of military dictatorships seemed to offer no real change, especially in terms of their need for land and peace.

The only change came from America, as we increased our troop commitments in support of governments which were singularly corrupt, inept, and without popular support. All the while, the people read our leaflets and received regular promises of peace and democracy and land reform. Now they languish under our bombs and consider us—not their fellow Vietnamese—the real enemy. They move sadly and apathetically as we herd them off the land of their fathers into concentration camps where minimal social needs are rarely met. They know that they must move or be destroyed by our bombs, and they go, primarily women and children and the aged. They watch as we poison their water, as we kill a million acres of their crops, and they wander into the hospitals with at least twenty casualties from American fire power to one Vietcong-inflicted injury. They wander into the towns and see thousands of children homeless, without clothes, running in packs on the streets like animals. They see the children selling their sisters to our soldiers, soliciting for their mothers.

What do the peasants think, as we ally ourselves with the land-

lords, and as we refuse to put any action into our many words concerning land reform? Where are the roots of the independent Vietnam we claim to be building? Is it among these voiceless ones?

False Liberation?

We have destroyed their two most cherished institutions: the family and the village. We have destroyed their land and their crops.
We have cooperated in crushing one of the nation's only non-
Communist revolutionary political forces, the United Buddhist
church. We have supported the enemies of the peasants of
Saigon. We have corrupted their women and children and killed
their men. What liberators!

Now there is little left to build on—save bitterness. And soon
the only solid physical foundations remaining will be found at our
military bases and in the concrete of the concentration camps we
call fortified hamlets. The peasants may well wonder if we plan
to build our new Vietnam on such grounds as these; could we
blame them for such thoughts? We must speak for them, and raise
the questions they cannot raise. These, too, are our brothers.

Perhaps the more difficult but no less necesssary task is to
speak for those who have been designated as our enemies. What
of the National Liberation Front? How can they believe in our
integrity when now we speak of "aggression from the North" as
if there were nothing more essential to the war? How can they
trust us when now we charge them with violence after the mur-
derous reign of Diem? And charge them with violence when we
pour every new weapon of death into their land? Surely we must
understand their feelings, even if we do not condone their actions. How do they judge us when our officials know that their
membership is less than 25 percent Communist and yet insist on
giving them the blanket name? They ask how we can speak of
free elections when the Saigon press is censored and controlled
by the military junta. Their questions are frighteningly relevant.
Is our nation planning to build on political myth again and then
shore it up with the power of new violence?

Here is the true meaning and value of compassion and nonviolence, when they help us to see the enemy's point of view, to
hear his questions, to know his assessment of ourselves. For from
his view we may indeed see the basic weaknesses of our own condition, and if we are mature, we may learn and grow and profit
from the wisdom of the brothers who are called the opposition.

So, too, with Hanoi. In the North, where our bombs now pummel the land and our mines endanger the waterways, we are met by a deep but understandable mistrust. In Hanoi are the men who led the nation to independence against the Japanese and the French. It was they who led a second struggle against French domination, and then were persuaded to give up the land they controlled between the thirteenth and seventeenth parallels as a temporary measure at Geneva. After 1954 they watched us conspire with Diem to prevent elections which would surely have brought Ho Chi Minh to power over a united Vietnam, and they realized they had been betrayed again.

When we ask why they do not leap to negotiate, these things must be remembered. Also, it must be clear that the leaders of Hanoi consider the presence of American troops in support of the Diem regime to have been the initial military breach of the Geneva Agreements concerning foreign troops. They remind us that they did not begin to send in any large number of supplies or men until American forces had moved in to the tens of thousands. Hanoi remembers how our leaders refused to tell the truth about the earlier North Vietnamese overtures for peace, how we claimed that none existed when they had clearly been made. Ho Chi Minh has watched as America has spoken of peace and built up its forces, and now he has surely heard the increasing international rumors of American plans for an invasion of the North.

A Voice to the Voiceless

At this point, I should make it clear that while I have tried in these last few minutes to give a voice to the voiceless in Vietnam and to understand the arguments of those who are called enemy, I am as deeply concerned about our own troops there as anything else. For it occurs to me that what we are submitting them to in Vietnam is not simply the brutalizing process that goes on in any war, where armies face each other and seek to destroy. We are adding cynicism to the process of death, for they must know after a short period there that none of the things we claim to be fighting for are really involved, and the more sophisticated surely realize that we are on the side of the wealthy and the secure while we create a hell for the poor.

If we continue, there will be no doubt in my mind and in the mind of the world that we have no honorable intentions in Vietnam. It will become clear that our minimal expectation is to occupy it as an American colony, and men will not refrain from thinking that our maximum hope is to goad China into a war so that we may bomb her nuclear installations.

Somehow this madness must cease. We must stop now. I speak as a child of God and brother to the suffering poor of Vietnam. I speak for those whose land is being laid waste, whose homes are being destroyed, whose culture is being subverted. I speak for the poor of America who are paying the double price of smashed hopes at home and death and corruption in Vietnam. I speak as a citizen of the world, for the world as it stands aghast at the path we have taken. I speak as an American to the leaders of my own nation. The great initiative in this war is ours. The initiative to stop it must be ours. . . .

I wish to go on now to say something even more disturbing. The war in Vietnam is but a symptom of a far deeper malady within the American spirit.

In 1957 a sensitive American official overseas said that it seemed to him that our nation was on the wrong side of a world revolution. I am convinced that if we are to get on the right side of the world revolution we as a nation must undergo a radical revolution of values. A true revolution of values will soon cause us to question the fairness and justice of many of our past and present policies. A true revolution of values will soon look uneasily on the glaring contrast between poverty and wealth. With righteous indignation, it will look across the seas and see individual capitalists of the West investing huge sums of money in Asia, Africa, and South America only to take the profits out with no concern for the social betterment of the countries, and say: "This is not just." It will look at our alliance with the landed gentry of Latin America and say: "This is not just." The Western arrogance of feeling that it has everything to teach others and nothing to learn from them is not just. A true revolution of values will lay hands on the world order and say of war: "This way of settling differences is not just." This business of burning human beings with napalm, of filling our nation's homes with orphans and widows, of injecting poisonous drugs of hate into the veins of peoples normally humane, of sending men home from dark and bloody battlefields physically handicapped and psychologically deranged, cannot be reconciled with wisdom, justice, and love. A nation that continues year after year to spend more money on military defense than on programs of social uplift is approaching spiritual doom.

This kind of positive revolution of values is our best defense against communism. War is not the answer. Communism will never be defeated by the use of atomic bombs or nuclear weapons.

These are revolutionary times; all over the globe men are revolting against old systems of exploitation and oppression. The shirtless and barefoot people of the land are rising up as never before. "The people that walked in darkness have seen a great light." We in the West must support these revolutions. It is a sad fact that because of comfort, complacency, a morbid fear of communism, and our proneness to adjust to injustice, the Western nations that initiated so much of the revolutionary spirit of the modern world have now become the arch-antirevolutionaries. This has driven many to feel that only Marxism has the revolutionary spirit. Therefore, communism is a judgment against our failure to make democracy real and follow through on the revolutions that we initiated. We must move past indecision to action. We must find new ways to speak for peace in Vietnam and for justice throughout the developing world, a world that borders on our doors. If we do not act, we shall surely be dragged down the long, dark, and shameful corridors of time reserved for those who possess power without compassion, might without morality, and strength without sight.

Rolling Stone Magazine Is Born

By Robert Draper

Amid the activism and social upheaval of the 1960s, rock-and-roll music was growing up. Much of the rock music of the era focused on shifts in societal norms and a new wave of independent thought that encouraged young Americans to challenge the status quo. Sexual experimentation, drug use, and a rebellious spirit were celebrated by much of the popular music of the time period, forming a definitive sound track for the changing face of American culture.

Jann Wenner, a native of the San Francisco Bay area, found himself at the epicenter of the societal and musical shift that gave rise to acts such as Jefferson Airplane and the Grateful Dead. An avid rock fan and aspiring journalist, Wenner formed *Rolling Stone* magazine in 1967, helping to embody this new wave of rock and roll. Wenner's magazine celebrated not only music, but the boom in cultural awareness. In an excerpt from his 1990 book *Rolling Stone Magazine: The Uncensored History*, author Robert Draper discusses the origin of *Rolling Stone*, sketches the talents of its creator, and comments on the importance of the magazine to American popular culture.

There are a million success stories in the annals of the baby-boom generation, none greater or stranger than that of *Rolling Stone* magazine. In 1967, a twenty-one-year-old Berkeley dropout scraped together $7,500 from family and

friends and started up a magazine. He did so because he was a
rock & roll journalist whose work no one else would publish;
also because he longed to meet his heroes: John Lennon, Mick
Jagger and Bob Dylan.

By the end of 1969, Jann Wenner's two-year-old *Rolling
Stone*—or simply *Stone*, as many affectionately called it in those
days—was generally accepted as the most authoritative rock &
roll magazine in the land. By 1971, *Rolling Stone* was what *Esquire* had been in the sixties and the *New York Herald Tribune* a
decade before that: the breeding ground of explosive New Journalists like Hunter Thompson, David Felton, Grover Lewis and
Joe Eszterhas. Two years later, the magazine began to make
money. Three years after that, it helped elect a President. By
1989, *Rolling Stone*'s parent company, Straight Arrow Publish-
ers, Inc., was worth perhaps $250 million—over thirty thousand
times its value twenty-two years before.

None of this would have been possible without a few key individuals: acidheads, anarchists, commune dwellers, social lep-
ers and parentless longhairs who loved music and feared the
morning sunlight. That having been said, *Rolling Stone* is a dis-
tinctly capitalist triumph. It prevailed because of entrepreneur-
ship and a dedicated labor force; because debts were overcome
and payrolls were met; and above all, because it satisfied a con-
sumer demand.

The latter was no casual feat, since most segments of society
had trouble figuring out just who or what the consumers were.
Political activists pronounced them the New Left. Establishment
journalists labeled them "hippies." Richard Nixon called them
"bums." Jann Wenner, in the meantime, believed that the only
common trait among this vast but amorphous constituency was
an abiding love for music. And so Wenner's genius dictated a
product that was as loosely defined and evolving as the generation it would serve. Its very nature was to avoid the set positions
assumed by its psychedelic and left-wing counterparts in the underground press. *Rolling Stone* would keep on rolling, advancing through the years and gathering no moss.

An Overnight Success

It thus became a generation's voice—perhaps the only trustwor-
thy voice; and for evidence, one need look no further than the
pages of *Rolling Stone* itself. Conceived during San Francisco's

Summer of Love, *Rolling Stone* championed a new pantheon of heroes—the Beatles, Dylan, the Rolling Stones, the Jefferson Airplane, the Grateful Dead, Janis Joplin, Jimi Hendrix—until its loving gaze was distracted by the marching, charging feet of National Guardsmen on college campuses. Then the magazine deepened with hot blood. Came a crooked President and a crooked new decade, and *Rolling Stone* stopped talking about love and revolution. New Morality met head-on with New Reality. From 1970 until 1977, no magazine in America was as honest or as imaginative as what Jann Wenner called his "little rock & roll newspaper from San Francisco." Greater truths were its aim. That meant toppling false idols of every denomination—from Nixon, the FBI and the Nuclear Regulatory Commission to Woodstock, Charles Manson and the Symbionese Liberation Army.

Even in the blandest of times, *Rolling Stone* published good journalism—sometimes great journalism, and often on subjects no other American publication could or would touch. Its writers, after all, were at least as disaffected as its readers. Most of them were deemed unfit for the conventional newsroom, and the rest passed their days thrashing about like salmon in an aquarium. *Rolling Stone* plunged them into deeper, faster waters. Years later, few would remember the origins of Michael Lydon (*Newsweek*), David Felton (*Los Angeles Times*), Hunter Thompson (*Jersey Shore Herald*), Grover Lewis (*Houston Chronicle*), Joe Eszterhas (*Cleveland Plain Dealer*), Timothy Ferris (*New York Post*) and Howard Kohn (*Detroit Free Press*). It seemed as if they'd never been anything other than *Rolling Stone* writers.

Not Just About the Music

They took up where Jann Wenner left off when the twenty-one-year-old editor wrote in his first column, "*Rolling Stone* is not just about music, but also about the things and attitudes that the music embraces." To a writer with a wild imagination, this was carte blanche. The music embraced irreverence, the fringes of American culture, lunacy in its most exalted forms, love, hope, fear, loathing. . . .

At bottom, however, *Rolling Stone* was about music. Often the magazine wandered from its central mission, but never for very long—sales figures always saw to that. Readers trusted *Rolling Stone*'s rock coverage, and so trusted even a writer like Grover Lewis, whose sign on his desk read: "I do not write no rock &

roll." The magazine seemed to understand *exactly* how important pop music was. Teen magazines trivialized it; *Crawdaddy!*, the first American rock magazine, placed it on high with the utterances of Plato and Aristotle; and the straight press scorned or ignored it.

Instead of defining rock & roll, or deifying it, *Rolling Stone* covered it—a truly revolutionary idea. Its writers interviewed Bob Dylan, John Lennon, Mick Jagger, Janis Joplin, Pete Townshend and Eric Clapton with the sense of purpose a *Time* reporter would bring to an interview with Henry Kissinger. Musicians were *worthy* news figures, proclaimed *Rolling Stone*, and their music was worthy of analysis. Readers often disagreed, sometimes vehemently, with the magazine's seminal critics. . . . In the end, however, these disputes were always welcome, for they upheld Jann Wenner's larger argument: The music matters.

Wenner's mentor and *Rolling Stone*'s co-founder, Ralph Gleason, often said, "Don't analyze it. *Dig* it." But Gleason, a brilliant man of a thousand opinions, also subscribed to the corollary: *Something not worth arguing about was not worth digging.*

Wenner's Talents

Perhaps *Rolling Stone* magazine grew out of an argument that was never settled.

It sprang, after all, from the restless impulses of Jann Wenner, America's most prominent editor/publisher of a magazine that does not feature nude women beneath its cover. Even those who despise Wenner rank him with the greatest editors of postwar American magazine journalism: Harold Ross of *The New Yorker*, Harold Hayes of *Esquire*, Clay Felker of *New York* and Warren Hinckle of *Ramparts*. If Wenner's agile mind does not approach theirs, his understanding of his audience and the tools at his disposal may have no equal.

"With the possible exception of Condé Nast," said Porter Bibb, who helped publish *Newsweek International* before becoming Wenner's first publisher at *Rolling Stone*, "he has attracted more talent than any other magazine publisher in this century. Furthermore, it doesn't matter what other editors you name: nobody had a better understanding of what was going on in this country in the sixties and seventies than Jann Wenner. And I don't think anybody's ever going to put together a journal that is as accurate a reflection of what's going on in the country as he did in *Rolling Stone*'s heyday."

Though he disapproved of his protégé's reckless business practices, Ralph Gleason nonetheless told a reporter in 1973, "He is a natural intuitive genius for this type of operation, whether you like him or not. If you gave me a million dollars to start a publication covering popular music and all aspects of popular American culture, I'd hire Jann. He's the best man for the job, period."

Gleason rightfully believed that Jann Wenner could not have pulled off *Rolling Stone* without his help. As with most great American success stories, luck had much to do with Wenner's ascendancy. *Rolling Stone*, in those critical early days that bury most new publishing efforts, enjoyed free office space and employees who were willing to work for peanuts. The record industry bankrolled *Rolling Stone*, advancing Wenner money after he'd drained the magazine's coffers on dubious expansion schemes. And musicians like Lennon and Jagger gave *Rolling Stone* their support long before it was obviously in their interest to do so.

But Wenner courted his good fortune. Like any of the great American entrepreneurs, from Henry Ford to Steve Jobs, the *Rolling Stone* editor had an indisputably brilliant idea. And he hustled to promote that idea, bearing the burden of his dream long after others would have laid it to rest.

His sales tools were peculiarly American. He was a vulnerable sort, pudgy and baby-faced, his inferiority complex plain for all to see, which made him a most unthreatening suitor. He charmed, he flattered, he eagerly played the fool. Like a child, he lacked any sense of history, and thus appealed to the child in everyone else with his starry vision of the future. These qualities did not translate well in crowds. But alone in an office room, one on one, Jann Wenner could spellbind with his boyish charisma.

Yet success is not always sweet beneath the candy coating. To implement his dream, Jann Wenner cut a multitude of ethical corners: stealing his initial subscriber list from another magazine, awarding himself shares of company stock so as to secure minority control, lying to advertisers about *Rolling Stone*'s readership and pocketing the magazine's subscriber dues while the rest of the staff worked for little or nothing. Those who have threatened Wenner in one way or another have lived to regret it. The man with the kitten's blue eyes will brawl in any ditch, personally soiling himself as no other publisher would, to protect his stunning achievement. Jann Wenner is a man of wealth and taste, but he is no gentleman.

From the very outset, Wenner proved his finest talent to be exploiting the talents of others. Absent any coherent method—his employee interviews often consisted of a single question, such as "What's your favorite Rolling Stones record?"—he hired individuals with virtually no experience and, as one of his former editors put it, "gave us enough space so that we could one day stand back and say, 'My God. I'm *good.*'"

An Unorthodox Staff

On the warped and wonderful *Rolling Stone* career ladder, an occasional short story writer like Tim Cahill, with, as he put it, "no idea how to be a journalist," could be dragged out of his classroom and assigned stories ranging from Ravi Shankar to Bigfoot. A teenager like Cameron Crowe could earn the right to pen cover stories long before gaining the right to vote. Reporters from underground papers became associate editors; writers became bureau heads; pasteup artists became production directors; graduate students with a good album collection became record reviews editors; a former animal caretaker became copy chief; an "office chick" who made the coffee became the magazine's research editor; and night switchboard operators and fact checkers could and did ascend to the rank of managing editor.

"We fix broken careers," Wenner would tell a reporter with a smirk. But he did much more than fix the careers of Joe Eszterhas and Howard Kohn, who left their newspaper jobs under disreputable circumstances; he let the reporters reinvent themselves as writers. Eszterhas now wrote about narcotics agents, Kohn about Patty Hearst and Karen Silkwood—just as David Felton dissected the violent cults of Charles Manson and Mel Lyman, as Grover Lewis pioneered movie reporting, as Tom Wolfe wrote about astronauts and as Hunter Thompson covered the 1972 presidential campaign. These articles were among the finest stories published in the seventies, anywhere. It is fair to say that most of them would not have been written, or at least printed, without the encouragement of Jann Wenner.

Wenner incited his writers to take risks and avoid niceties. Though many codes of conduct he simply found too time-consuming to abide by, others he honestly believed were foolish and hypocritical. Chief among these was "journalistic objectivity." If the gloriously disengaged Walter Cronkite was the antidote to radio's Ed Murrow and print media's Henry Luce, Wenner's *Rolling Stone* marked a return to engagement. The editor knew his readers. They wanted it told to them straight. Wenner urged his writers to scrape away the bullshit. If the President lies, call him a liar; if Dylan is a poet, call him one.

Though younger than many of his employees, the editor's uncanny focus lent him additional authority. For *Rolling Stone* staffers—many of them cut off from their conservative families and uncertain of their place in the world—Jann Wenner became a father figure. They loved him, feared him and did all they could to win his favor. At least as often as not, they wished he would go away. They huddled together at bars or smoked pot on the office rooftop, cursing their boss for his tirades and his eleventh-hour issue changes. Like any self-respecting father, he made their lives miserable.

"We were always hassling to keep Jann out of the running of the paper," said Charlie Perry, *Rolling Stone*'s first copy chief. "But that's also when *Rolling Stone* was great. . . . It made for fireworks, both on the pages and behind the scenes.". . .

The Original Fan

He was, as one of his former editors put it, "the original fan." It didn't matter all that much whether he was *seen* with stars. He simply wanted to *be* with them, to feel the glow of their charisma, to touch the sparks with his stubby fingers. Though he fantasized about becoming his generation's Henry Luce or William Randolph Hearst—the nickname Citizen Wenner was one he did not discourage—his own stature never preoccupied him as his surroundings did. Jann Wenner yearned to be in the company of greatness.

He reached for one constellation, then the next. As a Berkeley student he finagled his way into the debutante world. Then he discovered rock & roll. From Lennon, Dylan and Jagger he moved on to Tom Wolfe, Truman Capote and other vaunted literary figures. As politics captured his interests, he spoke now and again of running for office, some office or other. But that was never a serious prospect, even if one ignored Wenner's rather public history of drug consumption. No, Jann Wenner would settle for the company of greatness. Simply being there at those elegant Georgetown dinner parties was sufficient. . . .

The ultimate groupie, they called him. But Jann Wenner's own yearnings helped him understand the yearnings of his readers. In his heart, and in theirs, *Rolling Stone* wasn't the mainspring of cultural enlightenment. It was what he often said it was, to the annoyance of his subordinates: "a little rock & roll newspaper from San Francisco."

"My theory is this," said Jon Carroll, one of Wenner's early associate editors. "The reason that *Rolling Stone* was successful is the same reason that *Playboy* and *New York* succeeded: each was the complete encapsulation of a single person's fantasy. Hugh Hefner wanted to be a playboy, and Clay Felker wanted to live on the Upper East Side of New York City. Jann wanted to be with rock stars. And it turns out that each fantasy was shared by enough people to create a successful circulation.". . .

They are all gone now, the magazine's famous critics and music reporters and New Journalists and political writers and photographers and art directors—gone from *Rolling Stone* and dispersed among the American media. They now occupy critical positions at *Newsweek, New York Times, Los Angeles Times, Vanity Fair, GQ, New York, Playboy, Vogue, Manhattan, inc., Esquire*, ABC, MTV, ESPN and a host of local newspapers and television stations. They are respected professors and wealthy publishing consultants, noted authors and editors and literary agents, playwrights and movie producers, record company publicists and band managers. Among the nation's liberal arts community, they have ascended to the positions of greatest influence. They have become the Establishment.

Perhaps the fact that they were all there at *Rolling Stone*, under one roof, for a few utterly remarkable years, is the story most worth telling. But it tells only one side of the greater story.

"They'll all tell you the same thing," said Robert Greenfield, *Rolling Stone*'s London correspondent in the early seventies. "All any of us wanted to do was write for the people who read *Rolling Stone*. That's why I worked for fifteen pounds a week in London: because people that I cared about read *Rolling Stone*. They'd read my stuff, and it was straight across—it was *communication*. That's why we wrote, and wrote at the top of our ability. . . .

Perhaps because, in the words of former associate editor David Weir, "Jann doesn't have much conscience, but he has a lot of heart." To be sure, it was a strange game, this management technique of courting and bullying. But on certain levels, how could one dispute its effectiveness? An issue always went out, every two weeks. Novices and castaways did inspired work. *Rolling*

Stone was still a family, with all the attendant friction and heartache. The family endured. What choice was there? Outside slouched a far drearier world. This was life in italics.

"In a sense, I regret ever having met the guy," said Grover Lewis, who successfully sued Wenner over a breach of contract. "The experience left me feeling soiled and angry. But on the other hand: we *were* putting out the best fucking magazine in America."

Lewis often pondered that dilemma. He felt truly proud to be associated with a magazine conceived by a man he truly despised. Was *Rolling Stone* a minor miracle? A major tragedy? Perhaps neither. Perhaps, as Larry Durocher suggested, it was merely a man in print, with Lewis and the others serving as unwitting biographers.

"In the end, Jann's a brilliant master at getting what he wants out of people," said David Weir, who co-wrote with Howard Kohn *Rolling Stone*'s stunning Patty Hearst stories. "What he lacks is loyalty and trust. He's too insecure to allow strong people to grow up around him and therefore catapult the magazine to what it *could* have been: easily the most important magazine of our time.

"That's what Jann missed. He let the talent dissipate, let it go all over the place instead of holding it in one place as the repository of the sixties. Then you could have said, 'Goodbye, *Atlantic Monthly*. Goodbye, *Harper's*. Goodbye, *New Yorker*.'

"He missed that. *He missed that.* That was his huge flaw."

CHRONOLOGY

January 14: The Human Be-In, a hippie and counterculture gathering, takes place in San Francisco's Golden Gate Park.

January 15: The Green Bay Packers win Super Bowl I, defeating the Kansas City Chiefs 35-10.

January 27: A fire aboard the *Apollo 1* spacecraft at Cape Kennedy kills astronauts Gus Grissom, Ed White, and Roger Chaffee.

February 10: The Twenty-fifth Amendment is ratified, providing the procedure for empowerment of the vice president in the event that the president of the United States is injured or killed.

February 13: Canada denies entry in the country to LSD proponent Timothy Leary.

February 18: The National Gallery of Art purchases Leonardo da Vinci's painting *Ginevra dei Benci* from Liechtenstein for over $5 million, the highest price paid for a single painting.

March 12: Senator Eugene McCarthy of Minnesota, running on an antiwar platform, finishes second in the New Hampshire Democratic primary.

April 15: Large antiwar demonstrations take place in San Francisco and New York City.

May 2: Black Panther Party activists storm the California State Building armed with rifles and shotguns.

May 15: The Supreme Court establishes procedural protections for juveniles in court.

May 19: U.S. planes bomb downtown Hanoi.

June 5: Israel, Syria, Jordan, and the United Arab Republic begin the Six-Day War.

June 8: Thirty-four men are killed after the USS *Liberty* is bombed by Israeli aircraft during the Six-Day War. Israel claims the bombing was accidental.

June 12: In *Loving v. Virginia*, the Supreme Court declares that laws that prohibit the marriage of people of different races are unconstitutional.

June 16–18: The Monterey Pop Festival takes place in Monterey, California.

June 20: Heavyweight boxing champion Muhammad Ali is convicted of refusing induction into the U.S. Army and is eventually stripped of his title.

June 23–25: Soviet premier Aleksey Kosygin meets with President Johnson in Glassboro, New Jersey. They discuss arms control, the Middle East, and Vietnam.

July 12–17: Riots break out in Newark, New Jersey. In the six days of violence, twenty-six people are killed.

July 23–30: The Detroit riots break out. National Guard troops are called in to quell the rioting. Forty-three people are killed.

August 3: President Johnson announces that the United States will send up to fifty thousand more soldiers to Vietnam.

October 2: Thurgood Marshall becomes the first African American justice on the Supreme Court.

October 6: Residents of San Francisco's Haight-Ashbury district proclaim the "death of the hippie."

October 16: Three thousand marchers converge on the Oakland, California, induction center during the first day of "Stop the Draft Week."

October 21: Large antiwar demonstrations take place in Washington, D.C., at the Pentagon.

November 9: *Surveyor 6* makes a landing on the moon.

December 10: Soul singer Otis Redding dies in a plane crash.

FOR FURTHER RESEARCH

Culture and Counterculture

Muhammad Ali, *My Journey*. New York: Pan Macmillan, 2001.

Bob Cannon, "Burning Down the House: Jimi Hendrix First Lit Up America Twenty-Five Years Ago," *Entertainment Weekly,* June 19, 1992.

Sidney Fine, *Violence in the Model City: The Cavanaugh Administration, Race Relations, and the Detroit Riot of 1967.* Ann Arbor: University of Michigan Press, 1989.

Jane Gross, "Scars from 1967 Riots in Newark Are Still Visible in City's Central Ward," *New York Times,* July 13, 1987.

Abbie Hoffman, *Steal This Book.* New York: Four Walls Eight Windows, 2002.

Charles Jones, ed., *The Black Panther Party Reconsidered.* Baltimore: Black Classic Press, 1998.

Robert Love, ed., *The Best of* Rolling Stone: *Twenty-Five Years of Journalism on the Edge.* New York: Bantam Doubleday, 1993.

John Luce, "The Last Bad Days of Haight-Ashbury," *Esquire,* June 1983.

Michael O'Neill and Naomi Cutner, "Visiting the Revolution of Berkeley and the Bay; Where the '60s Were Born," *Life,* December 1984.

Charles Perry, *The Haight-Ashbury: A History.* New York: Random House, 1984.

Bobby Seale, *A Lonely Rage: The Autobiography of Bobby Seale.* New York: Times Books, 1978.

William Triplett, "Death on the USS *Liberty:* Questions Remain After Thirty-Five Years," *Washington Report on Middle East Affairs,* January/February 2003.

Juan Williams, *Thurgood Marshall: American Revolutionary.* New York: Times Books, 2000.

Space Exploration

Edmund H. Harvey Jr. and Erlend A. Kennan, *Mission to the Moon: A Critical Examination of NASA and the Space Program.* New York: Morrow, 1969.

Thomas J. Kelly, *Moon Lander: How We Developed the Apollo Lunar Module.* Washington, DC: Smithsonian Institution Press, 2001.

Vietnam and the Antiwar Movement

Michael S. Foley, *Confronting the War Machine: Draft Resistance During the Vietnam War.* Chapel Hill: University of North Carolina Press, 2003.

G. Louis Heath, ed., *Mutiny Does Not Happen Lightly: The Literature of the American Resistance to the Vietnam War.* Metuchen, NJ: Scarecrow, 1976.

Rhodri Jefferys-Jones, *Peace Now! American Society and the Ending of the Vietnam War.* New Haven, CT: Yale University Press, 1999.

John F. Kerry and Vietnam Veterans Against the War, *The New Soldier.* New York: Macmillan, 1971.

Mary Susannah Robbins, ed., *Against the Vietnam War: Writings by Activists.* Syracuse, NY: Syracuse University Press, 1999.

Thomas Alan Schwartz, *Lyndon Johnson and Europe: In the Shadow of Vietnam.* Cambridge, MA: Harvard University Press, 2003.

Randal B. Woods, ed., *Vietnam and the American Political Tradition: The Politics of Dissent.* New York: Cambridge University Press, 2003.

Websites

The Detroit and Newark Riots of 1967, www.67riots.rutgers.edu. Managed by Rutgers University, this excellent site offers images, history, and sound clips related to the riots in Newark, New Jersey, and Detroit, Michigan.

Hippies on the Web: Haight-Ashbury Music and Culture, www. rockument.com/links.html. Part of the Rockument Channel: Rock Music History website, this list of links covers various aspects of the Haight-Ashbury scene. Other information on the Rockument main page may also be helpful in researching the era.

Super Bowl Official Website, www.superbowl.com. The official site of the Super Bowl provides current information on the contest as well as some past history on the event.

Vietnam Veterans Home Page, www.vietvet.org. This site, run by veterans of the war, provides personal accounts of veterans, poems and stories written by veterans, and general information on Vietnam.

INDEX